No Shame in Wesley's Gospel

No Shame in Wesley's Gospel

A Twenty-first Century Pastoral Theology

EDWARD P. WIMBERLY

WIPF & STOCK · Eugene, Oregon

NO SHAME IN WESLEY'S GOSPEL
A Twenty-first Century Pastoral Theology

Copyright © 2011 Edward P. Wimberly. All rights reserved. Except for brief quotations in critical publications or reviews, no part of this book may be reproduced in any manner without prior written permission from the publisher. Write: Permissions, Wipf and Stock Publishers, 199 W. 8th Ave., Suite 3, Eugene, OR 97401.

Wipf & Stock
An Imprint of Wipf and Stock Publishers
199 W. 8th Ave., Suite 3
Eugene, OR 97401

www.wipfandstock.com

ISBN 13: 978-1-61097-193-5

Manufactured in the U.S.A.

The following persons were very instrumental in sustaining and mentoring me in my call throughout my college and football experiences at the University of Arizona in Tucson.

To: Rev A.A. Morgan, Pastor of Prince AME Church, 1961-64, who gave me my first oportunity to preach and who mentored in ministry;

To: Dr. Leland Scott, Director of the Wesley Foundation 1961-65, who helped to stimulate my theological academic interests formation; and

To: Mr. James LaRue, head coach of the University of Arizona football team 1961-65, to the assistant couches, and to my teammates, who taught me that my most significant contribution to the football team was to be an academic example for my teammates.

I remain blessed by them even today.

Contents

Foreword / ix
Acknowledgments / xi
Introduction / xiii

1. John Wesley's Theology for the Twenty-first Century / 1
2. Wesley's Therapeutic Model / 21
3. God's Present But Not Yet Future / 45
4. Wesley's Discipline for Guidance in Life / 62
5. Shame, Slavery, and Economics of Hope: Wesley's Public Theology / 78
6. Practical Public Theology: Civil Rights and the Wesleyan Spirit / 94

Bibliography / 111

Foreword

THE THEOLOGY OF JOHN Wesley has had a profound effect on the world through the United Methodist Church and five branches of African American Methodist Churches, as well as numerous nondenominational churches, and Pentecostal and Evangelical denominations who draw upon Wesleyan theology for ministry and doctrine. Although Wesley died in 1791, his insights into the emergence of a capitalistic society have significant value for today's world.

Whereas, in the past guilt was a primary focus for behavioral adjustment in theology, in the twenty-first century shame is (or should be) the dominant factor for shaping pastoral theology. Dr. Edward P. Wimberly does an excellent job of differentiating the two similar yet fundamentally different factors. Guilt is found in later stages of psychological development where an intact community exists with social and moral norms. In a guilty consciousness, the individual has a sense of being loved, being cared for, and belonging; therefore, when one acts against the norm, he or she feels guilt from not meeting the expectations of the culture. Shame is found in earlier stages of development before identification with a community can be established, where the self is totally dependent on others for love. In today's non-connected world where individuality and the fallacy of self-sufficiency is the norm, shame dominates when ones' attempts at success as measured by the world (status, wealth, power) are unsuccessful. In shame, there is a loss of community and a disconnected self-admiration where one feels unloved or at worse, incapable of being loved.

Wesley understood that as Christians we are citizens of two worlds – the "here and now" and the "present but not yet" coming rule and reign of God. Although Wesley's historical context in the eighteenth century is different from the twenty-first century, his views on wealth and riches can be extremely valuable today in a world where the devastating consequences of greed are evident. Just as Wesley used *rhetorical redaction* (the practice of taking Scripture out of its original context to apply it to a contemporary situation), Wimberly applies Wesley's thought to our current situation. Wesley believed that when we put our faith in God's "present but not yet" rule and reign then healing, wholeness, and happiness would result through a personal relationship with God through Jesus Christ. Being in relationship with God, people experience themselves as valuable, with worth and dignity. This is the cure for shame.

Wimberly continues by reviewing Wesley's healing theology and how Wesley's rhetoric was used and can be used to foster disciplined, holy lives. He then looks at Wesley's public theology including shame during slavery and its adaptation for twenty-first century Civil Rights and Liberation theology, bringing Martin Luther King, Jr. and James and Cecil Cone into the discourse.

This is an important work which brings the thought of Wesley into the pastoral theology of today. Only by dealing with the issue of shame can we bring the healing power of God to this materialistic "here and now" world. Wesleyan theology is an ideal place to begin the discourse and to look for solutions as we focus on the "present but not yet" coming rule and reign of God.

Rev. Richard D. Winn, Sr.
Senior Pastor
Ben Hill United Methodist Church
Atlanta, Georgia

Acknowledgments

WITH CONTINUED MATURITY AND experience, it becomes increasingly clear that creating a manuscript from its initial inspiration to its publication is a communal effort by a number of persons. I am indebted and thankful to so many persons.

First, I want to thank the members of my family, whose ongoing spiritual and moral support was and is essential in the production of a book. To my wife, my number one conversation partner in all publishing endeavors, I am so wonderfully blessed and grateful. To my sister, Pamela Wimberly Jones, who proofread and edited the entire manuscript throughout several rewrites, and to my sister-in-law Margaret Wimberly, who has proofread and edited most of my books over the years, I am thankful, for their commitment and prayers for me personally and for the work I do.

There are a series of scholar friends who are conversation partners and who have read and offered critical reflections and encouragements for my work in Wesley studies. They include Mark Ellingsen, L. Henry Whelchel, Russell Richey, Randy Maddox, Rex Matthews, Carol Helton, David Cann, and Brad Ost. There are a number of friends, colleagues, co-workers, students, and former students who share with me an interest in Wesley studies. They are Indonesia Wilson, Pamela Perkins, Cassandra Dorsey, and Tiwirai and Adlene Kufarimai. I am also very grateful to pastor Richard Winn at Ben Hill United Methodist Church, whom I asked to write the Foreword, and the members of the pastoral staff for their encouragement and for providing venues to test out my ideas with lay people. These persons include Michael Stinson, Gigi Warren, Jerome Wilder, Sam Townsend, and Agnes Harvey.

In addition to my local congregation, there were several people and venues who enabled me to test out my ideas. These people and places include Robert Jewett, who helped me to decide the title of the book when he invited me and my wife to lecture at St. Marks United Methodist Church in Lincoln, Nebraska. Dr. Angela Son, at Drew Theological Seminary, and Randy Litchfield, at Methodist Theological Seminary of Ohio, also invited me to do lectures on Wesley at their institutions, and in this way, helped to further the development of this book.

Indeed, to God be the glory.

Edward P. Wimberly
Interdenominational Theological Center
Atlanta, Georgia

Introduction

THE TWENTY-FIRST CENTURY IS historically different from previous periods, and therefore, pastoral theology must re-appropriate our faith heritage in ways that speak to the present in new and different ways. But, how may this happen? My goal is to show that Wesleyan theology, particularly the theology of John Wesley, offers a particularly helpful pastoral theological perspective for the twenty-first century.

This book focuses on how human beings experience the contemporary world today as compared to the previous historical periods. I attempt to explore how the theme of shame has shaped postmodern society and calls for a rediscovery of the communal nature of the church in order to speak to the needs of human beings. The book will show that shame is the dominant factor in shaping society in the twenty-first century, and this experience calls for a pastoral theology for addressing shame. As a Methodist from birth, I will demonstrate that John Wesley's theology of salvation is fundamental to dealing with postmodern shame. The focus on the relevance of John Wesley's theology for the twenty-first-century experience of shame is consistent with what is called Phase III of Wesley studies, namely examining contemporary issues in light of Wesley's characteristic theological convictions.[1]

THE EXPERIENCE OF SHAME

The experience of shame is a twentieth and twenty-first-century phenomenon. Here, experience is understood as a "state of mind" produced by personal and social forces and how they are interpreted.[2] Prior to the late twentieth century, people experienced guilt more persuasively than

---

1. Maddox, "Theology," 33.
2. Richardson and Bowden, eds., *Westminster Dictionary*, 204–5.

shame. Experience is all about how human beings participate in life and are impacted by it. Paul Tillich, a well-known systematic theologian of 1940s through the 1960s, set the stage for the discussion of experience in personal and subjective terms by using the concept of anxiety. For him anxiety was a general category describing human beings' awareness that they only had a limited amount of time to live on earth, and they had to make the most of life in the face of the threat of death or nonbeing. In fact, he believed that life was all about the "courage to be" in the face of the threat of non-existence and the threat of extinction.[3] He also believed that people experienced anxiety in terms of different states of mind, which were determined by historical and cultural location. One of these earlier forms of anxiety was guilt.

Tillich believed that human experience was characterized according to how persons experienced anxiety in different historical periods. These historical periods of anxiety included the anxiety over fate or death, the anxiety of emptiness and meaninglessness, and the anxiety of guilt and condemnation.[4] Anxiety as the threat of death was experienced directly as the loss of life; anxiety as the intimidation of emptiness and meaninglessness was experienced as the menace to our spiritual existence; and anxiety as guilt was a hazard to our moral existence.[5]

All three of these anxieties are potential negative forces at any time, but Tillich postulated that social and historical conditions determined which of these menaces became manifested.[6] For example, he said that anxiety and fear of death itself dominated life up until the Middle Ages, where the fear of condemnation, the fear of God's wrath, the fear of hell and guilt, and the fear of purgatory were prominent. The fear of condemnation and guilt dominated this period, and they existed up until the Reformation and the Enlightenment. During the Reformation and the Enlightenment, dominance shifted to the anxiety over spiritual nonbeing, or emptiness and meaninglessness. It moved from the domination of fear of death and feelings of guilt. The dominating hierarchical, social, and cultural control by the church and its doctrine was undone by intellectual changes initiated by the Reformation and the Enlightenment. Moral condemnation in this period was present, but it did not dominate.

3. Tillich, *Courage to Be*.
4. Ibid., 40–63.
5. Ibid., 40–41.
6. Ibid., 59–63.

For Tillich, however, the anxiety over spiritual non-being, emptiness, and meaninglessness dominated, while guilt and moral condemnation were still real.

Paul Tillich's assessment of anxiety was adequate up until the early 1950s. At that time social movements began to take place that introduced the need to expand the meaning of anxiety. In the 1950s and 1960s, the Civil Rights Movement and the freedom struggles against colonial rule in India and Africa began to manifest themselves. In the early 1970s, the social and political liberation movements took center stage, and the experience of being oppressed and in bondage to social forces and structures of evil became the dominant form of anxiety for racial and cultural groups; for women, who had been oppressed; for gays and lesbians, who were stigmatized as outcasts; and for the poor, who were being exploited. Those who experienced discrimination and were outcasts began to protest about their experience of oppression and began to desire liberation. Thus, the anxiety over being oppressed and exploited became dominant for oppressed groups. For some considered to be racially and economically privileged, however, anxiety could be called status anxiety, which is related to the threat of the loss of privilege, the loss of class status, the loss of wealth, the loss of power, and the loss of racial superiority.

Aside from status anxiety, there is another form of anxiety that is a late twentieth-century and early twenty-first-century phenomenon. It is the experience of the loss of love. Cornell West captured contemporary anxiety when he talked about the concept of nihilism. For him, contemporary life was characterized by the loss of meaning, the loss of hope, and the loss of love.[7] I characterize this form of anxiety using the concept of relational refugee.

> Relational refugees are persons not grounded in nurturing or liberating relationships. They are detached and without significant connections with others who promote self-development. They lack a warm relational environment in which to define and nurture their self-identity. As a consequence, they withdraw into destructive relationships that exacerbate rather than alleviate their predicament.[8]

---

7. West, *Race Matters*, 23.
8. Wimberly, *Refugees*, 20.

While the emphasis here is on the African American community, this experience of the relational refugee became a universal experience of all persons in western society. This was characterized by some of the following characteristics, known as the narcissistic epidemic, status anxiety, and the shame factor.

I have described the contemporary experience of shame in terms of three dimensions. The first dimension was status anxiety. I describe status anxiety in the following way.

> Shame in this lecture is defined as experiencing the loss of what society defines as worthy and valuable, and without possessing these symbols of worth and value, one is not loved and has no worth. In short, shame is the anxiety that, living without wealth, material prosperity, position, status, and power, one is unlovable and worthless.[9]

The second dimension is the experience of the self as a commodity to be bought and sold in the marketplace. The contemporary self is experienced as "an isolated and self-contained individual completely oriented to consumer and marketing values."[10]

The third dimension is a form of narcissistic or selfish self-admiration known as the narcissistic epidemic. It is typified as a gigantic fantasy with phony wealth built on "interest only mortgages" and debt, "phony beauty" symbolized by "plastic surgery and cosmetic procedures," "phony athletes" on "performance-enhancing drugs," "phony celebrities" due to multi-media and internet exposure, "phony genius students" depending on grade inflation, "phony national economy" built on massive government debt, phony feelings of being special built on false self-esteem, and all epitomized by the recent financial feltdown beginning in 2007.[11] Self-admiration, unlike self-actualization, is not experienced as being part of a relationship or community. Rather, it is experienced as being an individual who is disconnected completely from relationships. Moreover, self-admiration drives our economy, since our marketing efforts must convince people that they don't need relationships—but only material things, satisfaction of physical desires, and substances—to live a meaningful life. Thus, our economy is not

---

9. Wimberly, "No Shame," 105.
10. Ibid., 107.
11. Twenge and Campbell, *Narcissism Epidemic*, 4.

driven by the basic necessities in life, but it is driven by addictive impulses that lead to shame and self-destruction.

Given these three aspects of the experience of shame, I define shame in terms of the loss of love. It is the loss of meaningful community. It is the experience of being unlovable and the belief that one will never be loved.

The contemporary experience of shame is far different from the past experiences of guilt. Psychologically, guilt and condemnation come after the experience of shame in the developmental cycle, according to Freudian-oriented thinking. Guilt presupposes a more intact community where social values and morality are learned socializing principles. Shame, however, comes earlier in the developmental cycle, where the infant is totally dependent on parental and social relationships for love and affection. For example, in self-psychology, the self is developed primarily by internalizing significant others who make up the initial self, but who will later be differentiated from the self. Thus, the real self will emerge from the internalized relationships as an authentic self later in the developmental process. Frustration during the phase of internalizing significant others will be experienced as shame and the feeling of loss of love. In consequence, life is experienced as the anxiety of shame or of not being loved, with the belief that one will never be loved.[12]

THE SIGNIFICANCE OF JOHN WESLEY FOR THE TWENTY-FIRST CENTURY

Given the shape and form of shame in contemporary life—particularly in the western world and increasingly in the two-thirds world, including developing countries in South America, Asia, and Africa—what is the significance of John Wesley's theology for our contemporary age? To answer this question, we must understand that Wesley had a therapeutic and narrative-oriented rhetoric. For example, the quote below summarizes what I mean by his therapeutic rhetoric.

> Wesley's therapeutic rhetoric was based on his belief that happiness and healing of earthly spiritual, emotional, and interpersonal ills rested on a significant relationship with God through Jesus

---

12. The self-psychiatrist Leon Wurmser defines shame as the loss of love and the feeling of never being loved in *The Mask of Shame*. For the distinction between shame and guilt, see also Thomas and Parker, "Toward A Theological Understanding of Shame," 176–82,

Christ as well as significant relationships with the faith community. It is this emphasis on relationship that makes Wesley's ideas and rhetoric significant for dealing with twenty-first-century shame. Of course, a relationship with God through Jesus Christ was central to dealing with sin and the behaviors associated with sin for Wesley. The key element in Wesley's practical theology for this century is the fact that shame can only be healed through relationships. These relationships include the primary relationship with God as well as relationships with others.[13]

I am convinced that what we are struggling with in life are what is called mega-narratives or cultural myths that seek to motivate us to keep our economic system vital by orienting us and convincing us that our "identity, worth, meaning, and happiness are solely rooted in our total investment in this world's honor and shame system of evaluation."[14] This means that one part of our problem is that marketing is consumer driven, and the end result is we become commodities to be bought and sold on the open market. Secondly we are driven further by status anxiety. Wesley, however, lived during the eighteenth century, where he could see clearly that there was a new and changing mega-narrative that would lead human beings into bondage and destroy "our spiritual well-being and our souls."[15] Wesley provided us a narrative method of critically assessing the different cultural mega-narratives offered by society in light of a therapeutic and healing theology of salvation. Thus, this book is all about excavating Wesley's model of a therapeutic and healing theology of salvation, as a generative method of dealing with practical theology and ministry today.

Wesley offered a different vision of reality and of an opposing metanarrative. In the eighteenth century, the debate in philosophy and theology focused on whether happiness came from investing in spiritual realities or from those concrete things that could be confirmed by the physical senses, such as touching, hearing, seeing, smelling, and tasting. Wesley did not hesitate to join this debate, and he confirmed that there was one additional sense, which he called the spiritual sense. The reason behind his rhetorical stance was to persuade people that investing in the spiritual realm was the true source of our happiness, and the physical

---

13. Wimberly, "No Shame," 109.
14. Ibid.
15. Ibid.

senses should take their orientation from the spiritual sense. His gift to the twenty-first century is his belief that it was completely rational and sensible to put our faith in God's "present and not yet fulfilled future reign" and that when we invested in God's present and future, our healing, wholeness, and happiness would result.

Wesley believed in the "present but not yet quality of God's reign."[16] For Wesley, we live in this present world, but there is a future, perfect world, which God will transform in God's own way and God's own time. But, as we await the transformation of this world into a perfect world, we live by the power of the Holy Spirit and are empowered to live sanctified and holy lives anticipating God's future.[17]

While we are waiting expectantly for God's perfect world to unfold and living sanctified lives through the Holy Spirit, I add a contemporary plot logic scheme to Wesley's eschatological view of the future unfolding of God's transformation of the world. The world and our lives unfold like a literary plot in which there are stops, starts, setbacks, and temporary transformations, which make life meaningful. One of the major tasks of Christians who draw on the Wesleyan faith tradition is to declare loyalty to God's present but not yet future. This is done by critically evaluating the world we live in through the lens of the future transformation of the world that is on the way. More precisely, we must evaluate whether to invest our identity, worth, and value as human beings in the "enticements of wealth, prestige, status, position, fame, and public recognition," or to invest our lives in God's calling to participate in the present and not yet reality of God's rule and reign.[18] Clearly, holy and sanctified living through investing in the love of neighbor is consistent with living in the spiritual realm of God's future.

Wesley believed that Christians lived reality between two contrasting story plots. One was tragic, where human beings had to give up their souls in order to buy into this world's pursuit of wealth, prestige, honor, fame, or things associated with this world's honor and shame system. The other plot was positive and transforming, which invested in God's future and our ultimate happiness on earth as well as in heaven.[19]

---

16. Wimberly, "John Wesley and Twenty-first Century," 104.
17. Ibid.
18. Wimberly, "No Shame," 104.
19. Ibid., 110.

It is my strong belief that Wesley's gift to the twenty-first century is his therapeutic model of salvation, resting in his view that happiness comes from our relationship with God through Jesus Christ as well as our being empowered by the Holy Spirit to live sanctified lives of love of God and neighbor. This entire presentation in book form is based on this premise.

A CASE EXAMPLE OF APPLYING WESLEY'S NARRATIVE RHETORIC FOR TODAY

The relevance of Wesley's view for the twenty-first century became clear to me when I read a book by a family friend. His name is Glenn S. Henderson, a "sought after speaker and Christian leader."[20] He owns a very successful worldwide transportation and logistics company. "His example is of a person who developed his business rooted and grounded in being faithful to the 'present but not yet' unfolding rule and reign of God."[21] His book demonstrates that God had to divest him of his investment in this world's search for wealth before he could ever see any success in his business. In fact, his life with his wife and family went through many starts and failures until he finally realized that his business was not for his own success or his entrepreneurial image in the world. Only when he finally realized that God wanted his business to be Christ-oriented and dedicated to service of his neighbor did his company reach some stability. I say the following about his business ventures.

> Henderson admitted at that time he had no idea about the plans God had for his life. He quoted Jeremiah 29:11, saying that God knew the plans God had for him, "plans for his welfare and not for harm." God was about to use the Internal Revenue Service to bring lasting changes in his life and in the life of his future wife. God would use Glenn's and his future wife's business misfortune to edit and re-author their investment in this world's honor and shame system. They were about to learn that happiness was not in the investment in this world but in the "present and not yet" coming world of God. They had to go through hell, however, before they could make the new investment.[22]

---

20. Henderson, *Treasures of Darkness*.
21. Wimberly, "No Shame," 113.
22. Ibid.

It was not until Glenn and his wife Regina learned to trust God's "present but not yet future," and to give their lives over to trusting the Holy Spirit to guide their growing and living in response to God's sanctifying love of neighbor, that they developed a successful entrepreneurial endeavor. They clearly do not practice laying for themselves "treasures on earth." They live out the Wesleyan doctrine of "giving all you can."

THE ORGANIZATION OF THE BOOK

The outline of the chapters builds on the theology of John Wesley and especially his therapeutic salvation theology. Chapter 1 will explore Wesley's method of doing practical theology in the eighteenth century. The focus is on how he drew on doctrine, Scripture, and the intellectual ideas of his time period to persuade people that a relationship with God through Jesus Christ and the Holy Spirit was the major pathway to happiness in life. For him such a relationship was not only the source of personal happiness, it also was the source of Christian virtues and communal living.

Accessing Wesley's theology—particularly through his writings, which included his sermons, his tracts or treatises and notes on the Bible—involved understanding the non-coercive methods he used to influence people and the avenues people chose for pursuing happiness. Wesley's practical theology was largely rhetorical in nature, in that all of his writing, preaching, and his ministerial efforts seemed to focus on assisting spiritual formation, beginning with a relationship with God and Jesus Christ. Thus, his rhetorical methods of doing practical theology, whether in constructing liturgy, preaching sermons, writing commentary on the Bible, arguing with the intellectuals of his day, or writing treaties on public issues, all centered around persuading people about the primacy of a relationship with God.

After reviewing many of the rhetorical methods Wesley used to draw people into a relationship with God, the significance and relevance of Wesley's rhetorical approach to practical theology for the twenty-first century and shame will be examined. The conclusion of this chapter is that Wesley's rhetorical devices are not adequate for the twenty-first century unless they are updated by what is called narrative rhetorical thinking about God's involvement in history and life. The focus is on how rhetoric serves the ends of influencing people to join God's salvationist work in history, which is being carried out by God and to which God calls each of us to join. Wesley's view that happiness rested in being in relationship to God through Jesus Christ and the Holy Spirit also meant joining in doing God's work of love. Love is understood as joining God in God's works of love.

Chapter 2 shifts the focus to Wesley's therapeutic and healing theology. It is the contention that Wesley's therapeutic and healing theology of salvation is what makes Wesley's theology relevant for addressing twenty-first-century shame. Thus, there is a thorough examination of this healing and therapeutic theology and its relevance for today.

Chapter 2 builds on chapter 1's emphasis on rhetoric, but this chapter focuses on updating the narrative rhetoric already present in Wesley's thinking. Specifically, what chapter 3 does is to update Wesley's narrative thinking using twenty-first-century narrative theory. The focus is on what is called reframing of Wesley's narrative thinking for our current century.

Chapter 4 explores how Wesley's rhetoric was used to foster discipline and holiness in people's private and public lives. Here Wesley's therapeutic psychology, which focuses on the process of salvation as involving sanctification following justification, is examined from a narrative frame. This chapter also focuses on the reality that small groups are key places where people can find love and acceptance.

Chapter 5 and chapter 6 turn to Wesley's public theology and how he addressed the issues of shame during slavery as well as the implications of his theology for the twenty-first-century Civil Rights and liberation movements. Wesley was very concerned about race relationships, and his thoughts are relevant for this current century.

Chapter 1

John Wesley's Theology for the Twenty-first Century

In my essay entitled "John Wesley and the Twenty-first Century: A Realistic Future," I set out to demonstrate that Wesley's theology, which grew out of the eighteenth century, had relevance for contemporary issues confronting our society. The essay was grounded in my assessment that Wesley's theology responded to the rapid development of eighteenth-century modern capitalism. At that time, he struggled to address, for himself as well as for his own contemporaries, how to come to grips theologically with the increasing possibility of economic wealth resulting from industrialization. Moreover, Wesley sought to address the undermining impact of both economic wealth and an advancing intellectual movement, derived from Enlightenment influences, against the authority of the church. In my essay, I made the point that the consequences of the industrial era, and of the intellectual forces set loose during the Enlightenment, continue to be felt in today's society. Likewise, Wesley's theological wisdom has relevance for our contemporary culture. The essay sets forth the nature of the contemporary challenge.

In the essay, I draw on Wesley's theological wisdom as a means of addressing two problems facing the church, the nation, and the world. The first is the danger that the United Methodist Church's vitality will be diminished because of the neglect of its communal, small-group roots within local congregations, even as the church pursues its important and necessarily aggressive social agenda. Second, Wesley's theology will be drawn on for support in addressing a pernicious and deadly form of narcissism grounded in the pursuit of economic status, social status, and honor, which led to the most recent economic meltdown in the United

States and the world. In short, the essay sought to answer the question, "In what sense can Wesley be claimed as a source for theology today?"[1]

I want to make the claim here that the task for the United Methodist Church in the twenty-first century is one of mining the practical theology of John Wesley for our contemporary cultural problems. Indeed, I submit that this is not simply a concern specific to the United Methodist Church. It is a concern for all denominations that have drawn on John Wesley's practical theology for their doctrinal formulations, including pan-Methodist traditions or the five African American Methodist denominations, all churches within the Wesleyan heritages in the United States and abroad, Pentecostal and evangelical denominations as well as non-denominational churches that draw on Wesleyan theology, and other denominations that use Wesleyan theology in their understanding of ministry and doctrine. Toward that end, this chapter will provide a rationale for how to update Wesley's practical theology so that it can have relevance for today. This task recognizes that Wesley's theology addressed issues and concerns that were uniquely early modern in the sense that they were developments of capitalism. The church then was becoming more secular and was losing its authority in the marketplace. It is my belief that it is possible to bridge the gap between Wesley's time period and ours by identifying rhetorical practices Wesley used to address the situation of his time. When updated, his practical theological approach to the formation of persons in the faith especially has relevance for today. Therefore, this chapter is a methodological one. As such, it will lay the groundwork for what will be the task of this entire book. This task is to update Wesley's practical theology for the twenty-first century.

WESLEY AS A PRACTICAL THEOLOGIAN

Randy Maddox comments on the significance of practical theology by talking about the first and second order of theological reflection. For him, serious theological thinking takes place when the practical activity of ministry is reflected on theologically. He says that Wesley's gift to theology was being a practical theologian, and that his practical theology reflected the church's own understanding of doing theology when compared to what was taking place in the universities and academic communities.

---

1. Wimberly, "John Wesley and Twenty-first Century."

Wesley did theology by addressing two levels, according to Maddox. The first level was formational. It involved the basic and implicit assumptions shaping people spiritually, emotionally, interpersonally, and behaviorally.[2] For him this level of theological reflection develops as practitioners think about nurturing and forming people in their faith. Methods for influencing how people are formed and shaped by their faith tradition are developed. These methods include the production of sermons, catechisms, liturgies, manuals, tracts, treatises, and communal means of instruction. Maddox calls this level of theological reflection the first order of theological thinking. He says that this practical level sets the stage for the next level of theological thought.

For him, the next level of theological reflection is the grounding of these practical activities within a doctrinal framework. Practice always had to be grounded theologically. Wesley used pre-Enlightenment thinking for grounding practical theology. Pre-Enlightenment practical theology focused on the basic theological principle that happiness and virtue were found in relationship with God and that this relationship had all kinds of benefits and dividends for their growth and development.[3] Wesley's doctrine of salvation was the foundation of everything he did, and all of the church's practices served the goal of fostering a relationship of human beings with God through Jesus Christ. Moreover, being in relationship with God in Wesley's theology had the following benefits for persons. People experienced themselves as valuable with worth and dignity. They not only felt valuable, but were so delighted in the rewards of being in relationship with God that they sought to grow and develop their lives in accordance with God's guidance through the Holy Spirit. Theologically, the doctrines of justification and the assurance of salvation, the growth toward sanctification in love of neighbor, reliance on Scripture as a faithful and trustworthy guide, and growth and discipline in small groups, became the fundamental theological doctrines guiding practical principles of Wesley.

My reading of Wesley's primary sources indicates to me that he was very much in the pre-modern and pre-Enlightenment model of doing practical theology. Indeed, he followed the pre-modern methods. These methods used doctrine and Scripture to convince or persuade others that being in a relationship with God through Jesus Christ was the source of

2. Maddox, *Responsible Grace*, 16–17.
3. Charry, *By The Renewing of Your Mind*.

happiness. It was also the source of growth and development spiritually, emotionally, and relationally. Thus, practical theology for John Wesley was all about seeking to influence people to come into full relationship with God through Jesus Christ. This relationship would be nurtured in practices in small groups. Happiness was growth in salvation through holiness and love-oriented virtues.[4]

THE CASE OF GLENN HENDERSON

Earlier in this manuscript I introduced Glenn Henderson and how he pursued the riches of this world in his business and how he met failure after failure until he learned where his true happiness lay. The relevance of his story is that he lives in the twenty-first century, and life itself taught him that true happiness and the practices of Christian virtues began first with a relationship between himself and God through Jesus Christ. He believed that building his own life and business rested in his own hands. He gave no thought to the role of God in the process. Through his own hands, he was constructing his own world and his business. In fact, he writes, "I was busy building my house, a house on sand, a house built my way and a house without any foundations, values, purpose, character or even vision."[5] Eventually, through a process of discovery and participation in the life of Christian organizations, he came to the truth that is expressed in Palms 127:1, which basically points out that building a house is futile unless the builder is God. Thus, as he grew in his relationship with God through Jesus Christ, he learned that he had to build his life and business directed by God through the Holy Spirit.

In short, his life experience in the twenty-first century helped him to discover that happiness and salvation, even for contemporary people, still rested in a vital relationship with God. While he is part of a nondenominational tradition, Wesleyan practical theology's conclusion about the primacy of the God relationship is central to his, and to many, Christian churches.

WESLEY'S RHETORICAL METHODS

Wesley used a variety of methods to draw people into a relationship with God and to deepen their spiritual growth and development. These meth-

---

4. Wimberly, "Bible as Pastor," 65.
5. Henderson, *Treasures*, 104.

ods are called rhetorical approaches. By *rhetorical*, I am talking about the effort to persuade people to take a particular point of view.[6] One such rhetorical method is called invention. Inventions could include arguments presenting proofs, and proofs could be direct and indirect citations from authoritative sources such as Scripture.[7] It is clear that Wesley used invention often to make a point aiming to persuade others. His sermons are prime examples, and his treatises on specific topics are another example. In his treatise entitled "The Character of a Methodist," Wesley drew on scriptural quotes to convince readers that the unique characteristics of Methodists conformed to biblical bases, and these distinctive characteristics separated them from other Christian groups.[8] Exploring his methods of use of Scripture to help form and shape persons as they grew and developed in their relationships with God is important.

USE OF BIOGRAPHY AND AUTOBIOGRAPHY

Wesley used biography and autobiography inventively. For example, Isabel Rivers explored John Wesley's use of biography and autobiography to make his practical theological arguments. She emphasized that Wesley believed that individuals knew God through Scripture and through experience. She also said Wesley believed people needed the testimony of others in the process of coming to know God.[9] Wesley used the testimony of others in order to help people test whether their personal experiences cohered with the common experiences of others who were within the faith tradition. Wesley used biographies and testimonies also were used to encourage persons to continue to persevere in the faith. She pointed out this was Wesley's experimental method, and as a result of this method, he would systematically "collect biographies, autobiographies, conversion narratives, deathbed accounts—letters . . ."[10] This helped Wesley to test out his own ideas as well as to support his readers in their faith. About Wesley's use of testimonies from people's lives, Rivers went on to say:

---

6. Jewett, *Romans*, 23–42.
7. Ibid., 24.
8. Wesley, *Works*, 339–47.
9. Rivers, *Reason, Grace and Sentiment*, 205–53.
10. Ibid., 220.

His letters illustrate one way in which he collected this material. In the 1760s and the 1770s, for example, he was anxious to compile evidence of Christian perfection, and his letters are full of lists of questions to his correspondents about the details of their experiences. He explained one reason for doing so in a letter of 14 April 1771: "It is certain no part of Christian history is so profitable as that which relates to great changes wrought in our souls: these, therefore, should be carefully noticed and treasured up for the encouragement of our brethren." The other reason, to test the validity of a doctrine, is explicit in a letter of 11 June 1771: "I have lately made diligent inquiry into the experience of many that are perfected in love. And I find a very few of them who have had a clear revelation of the several Persons in the ever-blessed Trinity. It therefore appears that this is by no means essential to Christian perfection."[11]

The use of the testimonies of others to test one's own experience as well as to gain knowledge about doctrine was not only a substantiation of Wesley's rhetorical approaches to influence others, but it also spoke to his practical theological emphasis. Testing out one's experience against the experiences of others was what is called the method of coherence. Moreover, drawing from human experience to test out theological doctrine is also a theological method called analogy of being. More precisely, it was a way of testing out doctrinal statements against human experience. It must be noted here, however, that Wesley was not attempting to reduce doctrine to human experience. Wesley explored the meaning of Christian perfection in the lives of people against a Christian ideal. Rather than attempting to reduce Christian experience to the lowest common denominator, he was attempting to elevate the human experience of perfection to the highest possible denominator.[12]

WESLEY'S USE OF SERMONS PERSUASIVELY

Another rhetorical method used by Wesley was reflected in how he used Scripture to draw people into the life of living holily in a secular world. Wesley's sermons were simple in framework, and were organized to get the attention of the reader/hearer immediately. His introductions were short. According to George Lawton, he told the reader/

---

11. Ibid.
12. Ibid., 221.

hearer what he intended to do; he then did it; and then he told them what he had done.[13]

Another rhetorical feature of Wesley's sermons was Wesley's ability to make empathic connections with the reader/hearer. "The man who could on some themes let loose an avalanche of words, and upon other occasions move with logical precision, was also capable of describing human experience with clinical accuracy," says Lawton.[14] He had the capacity to be diagnostic as well as to assess the "soul's emotions."

Wesley's introductions were intended to get the attention of the reader/listener immediately and draw him or her into the world of the biblical text. In sermon 126, entitled "On Worldly Folly," Wesley invited the reader and hearer of the sermon into the parabolic story in Luke 12:15–21.[15] His rhetorical method was to invite people into the story in his sermon by first grabbing their attention. He began by saying that fools are commonly wiser in their own eyes than others who can render reason. Then, he went about trying to show that the man in the parable was foolish because he laid for himself treasures on earth and forgot God in the process. Thus, Wesley invited his readers and listeners to apply this story to their own lives.

I will continually use the joining of readers and listeners together since there is evidence that Wesley's written sermons were very similar in form to his extemporaneously spoken sermons. Commenting on the similarity between Wesley's outdoor preaching and his written sermons, George Lawton quoted Wesley's own words: "I now write, as I generally speak, *ad populum*."[16] This was not only confirmed by Wesley's own words, but also by those able to witness Wesley's preaching, particularly in the open air. Lawton reports that Rev. William Gurley recalled that on Sunday, May 1, 1785, Wesley spoke "a most able discourse, just the same as is printed."[17]

The significance of this sermon is not only for its insight into Wesley's rhetorical methods, but it also helps us to envisage how Wesley used sermons to foster scriptural holiness. First, Wesley allowed Scripture to do its own self-disclosure by encouraging the reader/listener to enter the

13. Lawton, *Wesley's English*, 240.
14. Ibid., 242.
15. Wesley, "Folly."
16. Lawton, *Wesley's English*, 247.
17. Ibid., 249.

story. Second, Wesley also reinforced his message in the story through expounding on the specific verses within the text. His rhetorical goal was to help the reader draw a parallel to his or her own life and world with the story in the text. Wesley's hope was that the readers/listeners would envision the limitation of this world and invest in the spiritual world that was present and unfolding in their midst. Indeed, this parable was what C. H. Dodd calls the "parable of the kingdom." That is, the kingdom of God in parables is the hope for the future as related to the reign of God. It is the eschaton or ultimate rule and reign of God.[18] It is God's sovereign power coming to rule in the world, and people need to be aware and ready as this reality is becoming manifest in the present. Evil will be overcome, and people will find fulfillment in relationship to God's presence and rule in the world.

Rhetorically, Wesley introduced the real problem that the text addressed. He focused on Luke 12:20—or the words "Thou fool!"—and he said he would explain these words. After that, he said, he would apply it to their consciences. The first rhetorical step was to get their attention, and the second step was to introduce the problem with which the text was struggling. The problem Wesley identified was the need for awareness of covetousness. He quoted Jesus' words about dividing inheritance: "'Beware of covetousness, for the life of a man,' that is, the happiness of it, 'does not consist in the abundance of the things that he possesseth.'"[19] Wesley used the technique of lifting up the dilemma of the main character in the parable by saying that this man did not know what to do with his abundance of crops. The man had a choice to share with relatives or to share his abundance with those in need. But, yes, he thought about what he wanted without first conversing with God. Therefore, Wesley showed how foolish the man was to tear down his old barns in order to build bigger ones, in order to secure his own future. That very night God required his soul. Thus, Wesley was using this story to draw readers/hearers into the story so that they would be persuaded, by the message, to produce the fruit of loving one's neighbor as the fitting activity for living in the world that God was transforming.

Of great significance was Wesley's use of poetic language to reinforce his message. He said: "See, Lord, how greatly my substance increases! Nothing less than thy almighty power can prevent my setting

---

18. Dodd, *Parables*, 23.
19. Wesley, "On Worldly Folly," 1:2.

my heart upon it, and being crushed lower than the grave!"[20] His poetic language appeared to be his own creation, sparked by his knowledge and understanding of Scripture, and this gift gave added rhetorical power to his message. His goal was to get the reader/listener to search his or her heart to ascertain where one's treasures lay, whether on earth or on the coming of God's reign. He asked: "Art thou labouring to be rich toward God, or to lay up earthly goods? Which takes up the greater part of thy thoughts?"[21] He then continued to warn the reader/listener to be aware of "covetousness; of decent, honourable love of money; and of a desire to lay up treasures on earth."[22]

This sermon was published in February 19, 1790, very late in his life on earth. The significance of this fact is that Randy Maddox identified this period as "late Wesley," which represented "a mature integration of the primacy of grace into his enduring concern for Christian holiness.[23] By studying the rhetorical method of inviting the reader/listener into the story, we are provided still another level of understanding of how to foster scriptural holiness. Wesley invited the reader/listener to participate in the story itself so that its power could draw the reader/listener to visualize himself or herself as part of the story and to identify with making the right choices about how to live one's life. Covetousness was, indeed, a problem for holy living, and Wesley enabled those in his reading and listening audience to envision the problem.

PERSUASIVE METHODS IN TREATISES

Wesley used sermons and biographies for the practical theological purpose of forming those within the faith community. Wesley not only focused on the faith community, but he also had to deal with those who were concerned about the challenges that his growing Methodist society movement presented to those within the Anglican Church. Therefore, he wrote treatises to clarify issues that were challenging for the Methodist society movement. One such issue dealt with the treatise "Character of a Methodist."[24]

---

20. Ibid., 2:2.
21. Ibid., 2:9.
22. Ibid.
23. Maddox, *Responsible Grace*, 20.
24. Wesley, *Works*, 340–47.

In "Character of a Methodist," it is important to understand the rhetorical situation in which Wesley was speaking. The *rhetorical situation*, in this case, refers to the fact that there were those in the reading audience who had raised serious questions that needed to be addressed by someone—Wesley—who was under public scrutiny. Wesley was often under the scrutiny of those in the Anglican Church and others who were suspicious of the motivation behind the Methodist society movement. For example, Isabel Rivers points out that the wider social context for understanding the Methodist movement and its rhetorical situation is the Evangelical Revival, which began in the 1730s and gave birth to groups she feels did not function in opposition to the established church but did cause much friction.[25] What caused the trouble was the fact that the Evangelical Revival gave rise to "irregular practices and structures (such as open-air, itinerant, and lay preaching, private chapels and meeting houses, religious societies, conferences, and connexions)."[26] These groups, according to Rivers, began to reinterpret their understanding of the doctrines of justification and regeneration in light of Reformation teaching. She emphasizes that one of the Evangelical societies was a group known as Methodists, and some were clergy within Anglican churches who felt that these groups were movements away from the established church.

There were other groups that opposed the Methodist movement who were largely secular. They were philosophical deists who emphasized reason and challenged revelation and the authority of Scripture.[27] Wesley's rhetorical situation included not only deists, but also included those who were called religious enthusiasts. These enthusiasts overemphasized faith, experience, and inward religion, while ignoring the law, morality, social holiness, and the behavioral ordinances of religion, reason, and human learning.[28] When thinking of the rhetorical situation in which Wesley was speaking, we must keep in mind the various conversation partners to whom Wesley had to defend the faith or challenge because of their distorted doctrine. His treatises, like "Character of a Methodist," were each only one such treatise in response to a particular situation.

25. Rivers, *Reason, Grace and Sentiment*, 206.
26. Ibid.
27. Ibid, 207.
28. Ibid.

From the very beginning of the "Character of a Methodist," the content of the essay gave the reader a clue not only to the rhetorical situation, but also to who the conversation partners were whom Wesley desired to address. From the onset of the essay, Wesley wrote that the distinguishing marks of a Methodist did not consist of opinions of any sort, nor a particular set of notions, nor the espousing of the thoughts of one person over another.[29] He charged that his opponents were ignorant of who Methodists were, and he pointed out that one of the distinguishing marks of a Methodist related to being Bible centered and focused. Wesley cited that the origin of Scripture was the inspiration of God. He said: "We believe the written word of God to be the only and sufficient rule both of Christian faith and practice."[30] He then indicated that he believed Christ was the eternal supreme God. After Wesley listed other characteristics that did not distinguish Methodists from others, he finally introduced what the distinguishing character of a Methodist was. He wrote:

> A Methodist is one who has "the love of God shed abroad in his heart by the Holy Ghost given unto him;" one who "loves the Lord his God with all his heart, and with all his soul, and with all his mind, and with all his strength." God is the joy of his heart, and the desire of his soul; which is constantly crying out, "Whom have I in heaven but thee? and there is none upon earth that I desire beside thee!"[31]

Wesley's response included several biblical passages. "The love of God shed abroad in his heart by the Holy Ghost" referred to Romans 5:5. The second came from Luke 10:27 and Mark 12:28–30, which referred to the summary of the Decalogue. He also quoted Psalm 83:25 and 73:25 referencing God as the desire of one's heart. Wesley also focused on other biblical themes that he felt were marks of a Methodist, which included happiness in relationship with God, and which referred to a hymn he translated from Spanish into English whose first line was "O God, my God, my all Thou art!"[32] This essay also addressed finding redemption and forgiveness (Isa 4:22); being justified (Rom 3:24–26); knowledge that one is a child of God (Gal 4:6 and Rom 8:16); being

29. Wesley, *Works*, 340.
30. Ibid.
31. Ibid., 341.
32. See "O God, My God, My All Though Art!"

born in hope (1 Pet 1:3–4); being full of immortality (1 Thess 5:18); being empowered by the Holy Spirit and loving neighbor as oneself (Matt 22:39); having a pure heart, loving not the things of the world, and fixing ones eyes totally on God. Wesley then said: "If any man say: 'Why, these are only the common fundamental principles of Christianity!' thou hast said."[33] And Wesley confirmed that this was correct, and that he taught only plain Christianity, and he said he renounced and detested all other marks of distinction.

In the conclusion of his essay, Wesley offered his right hand of fellowship to his conversation partners, and he exhorted them to walk worthy of their calling. In fact, the ending of the essay read like a conclusion to one of Paul's letters to one of his churches.

The significance of Wesley's essays and treatises was not just limited to his conversations within the established church or other Christians. As indicated above, he also was a public figure who had conversation partners who were philosophers, politicians, intellectuals of his day, and others. The key is to realize that Wesley's gift, as a practical theologian, was that his world included the formation of persons within the church as well as his defending the faith to those outside of it. He also fashioned his rhetorical methods of persuasion to take full advantage of his knowledge of the social and cultural location of his audience.

To summarize this chapter thus far, Wesley's focus, from a rhetorical perspective, was on the rhetorical situation and the narrative world that lay behind the conversations and discourses, and Wesley always geared his writings to his audience and conversation partners. The rhetorical situation fed Wesley's intent to address the things his audience needed, including the use of Scripture.[34] The narrative situation in Wesley's case consisted of the dominant contemporary conversations or discourses taking place, and Wesley found ways to make his argument for or against certain perspectives in his writings. The point is that Wesley lived in a dynamic world of ideas, and he continually defined his ideas in contrast to the ideas of others. For example, Wesley consistently emphasized the contrast between the spiritual world that was unfolding with the reign of God and the material and earthly world that was in opposition to the rule and reign of God. Another example was Wesley's development of his ideas as he matured over the years, from his early ministry to his later ministry.

33. Ibid., 346.
34. Jewett, *Romans*, 41.

THE CONTEXT OF WESLEY RELATING SCRIPTURE TO PEOPLE

Identifying the situational location of Wesley's conversation partners is essential for getting clarity about the actual meaning of what Wesley was conveying, through speaking and writing, to his original audience. He knew the situational context of his audiences, including their social and cultural backgrounds, the intellectual philosophies of the time, political agendas, and the professional practices of ministerial and secular professions, which all lend themselves to reconstructing the original settings in which he spoke.

John Wesley was university trained, and he was certainly trained to understand the methods and practices attending to reading the Bible in Greek and Hebrew. In fact, he sought to use scriptural language in a way that was consistent with the spirit of biblical language as well as with the letter of biblical language.[35] Yet while he was familiar with attending to the original meaning of the Greek and Hebrew words in the Bible, he was not bound by the biblical context of the original words. He also practiced with considerable license the art of rhetorical redaction. *Rhetorical redaction* is the practice of taking Scripture out of its original context and applying it to one's contemporary situation.

DRAMATIC INVENTION

Wesley had the ability to employ the language of Scripture, and he made it come alive in the lives of those who heard him and read his works. For example, through the skilled use of the English language Bible, and by employing the present tense, he drew listeners and readers into the scriptural text and into the drama and the story behind the text.[36] Wesley would make Scripture dramatic and would quote it in ways whereby the reader/listener took on a role within the text. John Lawton says the following about Wesley:

> He had a special aptitude for employing the language of Scripture in the form of direct speech. He seldom wrote such things as "We read in the Bible" or "Let us turn to examine the evidence of Scripture"; he makes Scripture the living utterance of his dramatis personae. Often this is indicated by

---

35. Lawton, *Wesley's English*, 94.
36. Ibid., 170–72.

quotation marks in the manner of the novelist; often the case is otherwise.[37]

Lawton later continues by describing the rhetorical method of what he calls "Scripture dialogue" in Wesley's sermon "The Good Steward." He talks about how the sermon contains lengthy "dialogue in a dramatization of the Judgment Scene."[38] Lawton quotes a lengthy part of Wesley's use of rhetorical invention where, rather than quoting Scripture exactly as it appeared in the English translation, Wesley inserted the voice of the listener/reader into the judgment, whereby which the reader/listener actually became part of the dramatization. Lawton points out that Wesley's rhetorical invention of "quoting" Scripture to make a point would be conventional if Wesley quoted the English text accurately. As a result, Lawton says: "To call this kind of thing 'quotation' of Scripture is most unsatisfactory."[39] Yet, Lawton describes the rhetorical technique as employing a living voice which spoke to the listener/reader. Wesley used the present tense, indicating that God's voice lived, and the listener/reader was encountering the living voice of God. He said that Wesley not only had God speaking in the living voice, but that God endowed the characters in the text with a living voice.

I am reminded of my local congregation where Scripture is dramatized by a group of congregational actors whose group is called The Word Made Flesh. Like this group, Wesley contemporized the word of God in dramatic fashion for his reading and listening audiences. I agree with Lawton when he says that "the Sermons teem with passages which, paradoxical though it may seem, are rhetorical and yet at the same time intimate and personal."[40] He says that the reader/listener cannot "escape being a participant in the dialogue."[41]

While Lawton uses the concept of scriptural dialogue to describe Wesley's use of rhetorical invention, I would like to introduce a substitute rhetorical concept, which I call proleptic (prolepsis) invention. The principle of prolepsis means real anticipation of the future. It relates the

---

37. Ibid., 170.
38. Ibid.
39. Ibid., 171.
40. Ibid., 173
41. Ibid.

Old Testament's expectation of God's future in both the Old and New Testaments.[42]

Wesley used the method of drawing the readers and hearers into the specific biblical stories, and this method of enabling them to participate in the biblical story as characters has another dimension to it. They also encountered God's unfolding story of salvation, and this story initiated them into God prolepsis or God's hopeful future. Encountering this future provided them with a contemporaneous experience of God's presence and the benefits of God future reign. The benefits of the future included health, healing, wholeness, and happiness.

This initiated the reader not only to God's unfolding story of salvation and God's reign on earth, but it also facilitated the use of *biblical plot logic*. Biblical plot logic is the language of hope that lies behind the entire Bible, where God works out God's redemptive plan for the world within the context of the cosmic struggle with Satan. Biblical plot logic is not the Grecian comic or romantic logic of positive and happy endings. Nor is biblical plot logic tragic or ironic plot logic where endings are always dead ends or where everything turns to naught. Rather, biblical plot logic is eschatological logic where God works out God's plans for the redemption of the world despite the presence of pain, suffering, evil, and interruption. Biblical plot logic from the standpoint of prolepsis reflects the logic expressed in Jeremiah 29:11: "For I know the plans I have for you, says the Lord, plans for your welfare and not for evil, to give you a future and a hope."[43]

Biblical plot logic is a proleptic way of talking about the work of grace in the believer's life that not only enables him or her to experience God's transforming grace in the present, but also initiates him or her into God's glory when the world is finally transformed at the end of time. It is plot logic that helps to make sense of what Wesley called justifying and sanctifying grace. It also helps to make sense of Wesley's holistic emphasis on the need for good works through sanctification to supplement the work of justifying grace.

It is my conclusion that in Wesley's use of what Lawton called scriptural dialogue—where readers/listeners were drawn to participate in the text—Wesley was also utilizing proleptic invention. That is, it was Wesley's way of making Scripture alive and relevant to the readers/listen-

---

42. Richardson and Bowden, eds, *Westminster Dictionary*, 472.

43. May and Metzger, eds., *New Oxford Annotated Bible (RSV)*.

ers through dramatized participation. It was also forming his readers/listeners into participants in biblical plot language, which enabled them to interpret and reframe their lives as if unfolding chapters in a book. In short, plot logic is narrative logic where the dramas of life unfold one scene and one chapter at a time. Behind these unfolding scenes and chapters of the book, God is working out God's plan. Our journeys on earth are not useless or dead ends. God is taking us somewhere, and on the way, we are urged by Wesley to secure our relationship with God.

THE RELEVANCE OF WESLEY FOR THE TWENTY-FIRST CENTURY

Randy Maddox employed the concept of responsible grace to explain the organizing principle of Wesley's practical theology.[44] This concept focused on Wesley's concern for the nature of God's action. God's gracious gift of forgiveness and empowerment enabled humans to be responsible.

My concern with Wesley as a practical and pastoral theologian is the relevance of his theology to our contemporary society, which is preoccupied with narcissistic self-admiration and status anxiety. The narcissistic epidemic, the age of entitlement, and the age of shame and of status anxiety have thoroughly permeated our political and economic structures of our capitalistic society. Our consumer, marketing, and commodity practices are out of control, leading to unchecked abuse of power. A massive transformation of our contemporary worldview is needed. Wesley's view regarding personal transformation, the necessity of small group participation, and nurturance will play a major role in our public life. We need to reevaluate the role of small groups in our public life and not just concentrate our work at the General, Annual, and Jurisdictional Conference levels alone in the United Methodist Church. The local congregations and small groups within them are keys to renewing structures for facilitating political action and social participation, as many political scientists are realizing.[45]

The attention to rhetoric gives us a clear picture into Wesley's attempt to use his speaking and writing to form and shape the worldviews of those many people who set in motion this movement called

---

44. Maddox, *Responsible Grace*, 19.

45. Black political scientists have noted that an increase of personal agency among African Americans has led to political participation to address the needs of others. See Wimberly, *African American Pastoral Care and Counseling*, 61–78.

Methodism. His rhetorical practices and strategies are key vehicles that can be used to impact and influence the worldviews that shape the lives of people and congregations. Thus, the rhetorical methods of Wesley outlined in this chapter will be prominently drawn on in later chapters.

Wesley's theological vision, which envisages the role of rhetoric as helping to draw people into unfolding and hopeful biblical plot, will be central for making Wesley relevant to the twenty-first century. Rhetorical plot strategies are essential for the church to employ, in small groups within congregations, to facilitate personal and social transformation. Here, rhetorical plot strategies are consistent with the methods Wesley used, in small groups, when he worked with poor children as his outreach from the Oxford Methodists movement, early in his ministry. These methods included biblical storytelling, praying, and teaching the truth of the faith.[46]

To make Wesley's practical theological approach relevant for the twenty-first century, it is necessary to reframe Wesley's concerns for the danger of riches by drawing on contemporary narrative theory, namely plot logic. More precisely, it is important to deal with the culture of narcissism and status anxiety that dominates human desires and relate to the nature of sin, which not only has personal implications but also political, socio-cultural, and economic dimensions.

Another implication of this chapter is to employ the rhetorical technique called redaction. Redaction was a technique used by the New Testament biblical writers as they attempted to reinterpret ancient Old Testament writings to fit a new situation.[47] The point is that Wesley's historical context in the eighteenth century is different from our context in the twenty-first century. His concern about wealth and riches were important when he developed his ideas, within the context of an emerging industrial and technological, modern revolution. The difference between Wesley's historical context and our historical context is that we are witnessing the most devastating consequences of allegiance to economic materialism in this Bernie Madoff era of complete lack of conscience in swindling thousands of people out of billions of dollars. Wesley's doctrinal ideas related to sin are still relevant, but they must be edited to fit a new situation.

---

46. Marguart, *Wesley's Ethics*, 19–21.
47. Jewett, *Romans*, 1018.

Another way to employ the rhetorical form of redaction is to explore the nature of plot logic used by Wesley's contemporaries and those with whom we enter into discourse today. For example, the plot of therapeutic salvation during Wesley's time assumed that human beings were communally connected. Such an assumption cannot be made today. The communally connected self must be contrasted with our contemporary emphasis on the disconnected self rooted in disconnected self-admiration.

The capitalism Wesley saw developing was far different from the economic system in place today.[48] Moreover, Wesley's society was driven more by what we call a guilt orientation, which largely focused on behavior. A guilt orientation assumes a relatively secure sense of self-worth where the self is relatively connected communally. In a guilt orientation, individuals have a sense of being loved and cared for by others—although the authoritarian discipline of the time could be overwhelming. The reality today, however, is that we can no longer assume in human beings a guilt orientation, which assumes a communal connection. The feeling of guilt is much less of a factor in personal and spiritual formation than during Wesley's era. Today, shame is more prevalent in the formation of persons than the feeling of guilt.

Speaking to the twenty-first century, pastoral theologians spell out how the experience of shame is more prominent today than the experience of guilt. "Shame is developmentally prior to guilt," say two pastoral theologians, based on Erikson's model.[49] Shame, on the one hand, is all about the developing self and how, to develop a sense of self, children internalize significant others. Guilt, on the other hand, is all about an already developed self. The most dramatic example of this in my early ministry was a young woman with insufficiently internalized significant others. She allowed herself to enter into very destructive relationships in order to be loved. In fact, there was very little guilt about the kinds of things she did in order to be loved, until, through counseling, she felt affirmed and loved. At that point, she had a more developed sense of self, and she then began to have guilt over the ways she had sought love.

---

48. See a description of the developing stages of the Industrial Revolution in Marquardt, *Wesley's Ethics*, 24.

49. Thomas and Parker, "Toward A Theological Understanding of Shame," 178.

"Shame not guilt is now the dominant debilitating emotion with which those in western culture struggle."[50]

Contemporary shame is all about the loss of the communal dimension, and it is a persistent feeling individuals have that they are not loved and will not ever be loved. Shame is real, and is the motivation behind many of the problems related to disconnected self-deficiency that we experience today. Disconnected self-deficiency cannot be resolved without participating in small groups where people feel loved and embraced by others. In Wesley's day, people sought to flee from the snooper-village where behavior was scrutinized and guilt applied; whereas, today, the escape from the village has become the manufacturing of shame or the feeling of never being loved.

To summarize, in this book, the rhetorical method of redaction will be used to help make Wesley's thinking about doctrine relevant for our current age. The term *redaction* is often used in biblical studies to refer to taking ideas from another context and using them for other contexts. Thus, Wesley's theology on riches, for example, will be employed to address the needs of people living in the twenty-first century.

Moreover, Wesley's understanding of the small group and its pastoral role in shaping persons can be redacted for addressing the shame of not being loved. More precisely, feeling unloved and uncared for drives our contemporary behavior. This feeling is related to the pursuit of self-admiration and the honor of being wealthy, the result of thinking that wealth and fame are the source of love. Wesley's view that happiness rested in God alone is the central message that must be conveyed in this narcissistic and status-oriented world. The small group experience is the crucible where human beings can be formed in their relationships with God and with each other.

Finally, I conclude that Wesley's effort to persuade persons that a relationship with God resulted in earthly and eternal happiness as well as in virtuous living is what we can glean as Wesley's message for the twenty-first century. His healing and therapeutic model of salvation, with its focus on the growth of human beings grounded in a relationship with God through Jesus Christ and nurtured in small group relationships for the purposes of growing in love of neighbor, is what makes his practical and pastoral theological model relevant for today. Indeed, we use the rhetorical redaction in that we take his healing and therapeutic

50. Ibid., 176.

model from his eighteenth-century context, which addressed the primary experience of guilt, and apply it our twenty-first-century experience of shame. We will update it, utilizing contemporary, narrative-oriented, practical pastoral theology.

Chapter 2

Wesley's Therapeutic Model

INTRODUCTION

THE AIM OF THIS chapter is to help discern the relevance of John Wesley's theology for the twenty-first century. Toward this end, I draw on a pastoral theological method, which brings to bear on our faith tradition current and contemporary knowledge and wisdom emerging out of pastoral practice. Much of pastoral practice today privileges the shame psychological model rather than the guilt model. Thus, the essay lifts out the thinking of Wesley that relates to the twenty-first-century experience of shame. The results of study of selected sermons of Wesley reveal that he addressed both shame and guilt, and his therapeutic and healing theology of salvation speaks potently to contemporary issues of shame. Shame is understood as being alienated from community, which produces a sense of being unloved, and people often seek social status and material wealth to satisfy the resulting need for love. The implications of this examination for a model of pastoral theology for the twenty-first century will be addressed.

THE CASE OF GLENN HENDERSON

Glenn Henderson is our twenty-first-century barometer regarding whether Wesley's practical theology has relevance for today. He is an African American, married male, who is a very successful entrepreneur and whose success in a worldwide transportation business did not take place until he gave up his efforts to seek happiness through the prism of seeking treasures on earth and sought to find it by giving his heart, his personal relationships, and his business over to God through the power of the Holy Spirit. Since that time, his sole purpose has been to execute his business as a steward of God's resources. In fact, the business is not his, but a gift of God, over which he is responsible, to make sure that God's glory and love is manifest.

Glenn's current happiness, however, did not come easy. In fact, he tried and tried, over and over again, to make his business work. He pointed out that, "living with pride as a best friend, [he] did not realize that pride blinds."[1] He made decisions that were reckless and stupid. Pride blinded him to who he was as a person as well as to the fact that he was heading for a fall and a failure that would lead to shame and ridicule.

Eventually, his world collapsed around him, and he pointed out that he recalled "realizing that [he] was being humbled and that [his] pride" and his failure was exposed.[2] He was "exposed as being incompetent"; he lost everything; he let others down; and, he said, "virtually everything [he] started failed."[3] In short, he experienced a twenty-first-century sense of shame in that his failure was public, but it also alienated him from those for whose lives he was responsible. To a certain extent, he became a relational refugee, cut off from others because of his pride.

Yet, his guilt, for his pride and for his arrogance in trying to develop his business without God, and his shame, at being a failure cut off from a community of working colleagues, were not too severe for God's healing and therapeutic love and grace. He said that he did not actually hear about God's love and compassion or how God understood what he was going through. Yet, in 1982, "broken, lost, disillusioned, and in dire need of help," God found him and his wife; they became whole. He said: "There was somebody who knew me in all of my shortcomings and in knowing me still loved me and accepted me."[4]

Later in this chapter, the reader will envisage clearly how relevant Wesley's healing and therapeutic theology is for today. Clearly, Glenn's testimony and witness will help us see just how relevant it is.

---

1. Henderson, *Treasures*, 132.
2. Ibid., 136.
3. Ibid., 153.
4. Ibid., 157.

THE CONTEMPORARY TASK OF PASTORAL THEOLOGY

The task of theology, according to Marjorie Suchocki, a Wesleyan studies scholar, is to bring to bear on tradition much of the knowledge and scholarship of the present. Such a task is one of adaptation, and it is necessary for every generation to make tradition relevant for today. She points out that Wesley did the very same thing for his own age.[5] Similarly, pastoral theology has a related task. It identifies, from practice and experience with people undergoing pastoral counseling and care, twenty-first-century issues to which theology must speak. Thus, the experience of shame is one of the major twenty-first-century problems to which theology must speak.

The goal of this essay is to draw, from Wesley's integrated juridical guilt and the therapeutic model of salvation, possible implications for responding to contemporary shame issues. The aim is to update Wesley's eighteenth-century theological thinking about salvation and to bring it to bear on the twenty-first-century experience of shame.

PASTORAL THEOLOGY AND SHAME

Shame is clearly a twenty-first-century issue. In the mid 1980s, pastoral theologians John Patton and Don S. Browning began to reflect on the problems of shame that counselees brought to pastoral counseling. These two pastoral theologians clearly make shame psychology a twentieth-century development.[6] To the mind of Patton, shame is a twentieth-century reality because it is a dominant experience different from guilt. To him, shame includes the entire self, whereas guilt includes only behavior. Shame is experienced as a negative self-evaluation resulting from pained interpersonal relationships, and guilt is more related to moral transgressions, which require moral and behavioral treatment.[7] Shame involves the self and its worth and value, and it is associated with not being loved and the hurt that results from feeling rejected and unloved. This shame is infectious and contaminates the entire self in ways that guilt does not.[8]

---

5. Suchocki, "Wesleyan Grace," 540–53.

6. See John Patton, *Is Human Forgiveness Possible*. See also Don S. Browning, *Thought and Psychologies*.

7. Patton, *Is Human Forgiveness Possible*, 40–53.

8. Ibid, 13–14.

Browning also envisages shame as involving negative self-evaluation, and he examines how shame is grounded in the shifts in social, cultural context evident in the shifts of clinical populations. He notes that the classical Freudian psychological approaches to therapy in the late nineteenth century and the early twentieth century, which focused on neurotic personalities struggling with Oedipal problems, had changed. He describes the shift from a guilt-oriented culture to a shame-oriented culture. For him, the neurotic culture was characterized by a "guilty man" who was "constantly infringing upon the rights of others in an effort to satisfy his (her) own insatiable appetites."[9]

Contrasting the guilty man, however, was the twentieth-century tragic man. The tragic man was one who experienced the loss of love, empathy, and parents. For him, the Freudian myth of Oedipus, which sought to kill authority represented by the father, was no longer the appropriate story or myth for a new century. Rather, more appropriate for the twentieth century was the myth of Odysseus and Telemachus. This is a myth or story about missing parents and the need for surrogates and mentors to replace parents in a parentless generation.[10]

What separates the guilt-oriented culture from the shame-oriented culture is the dominant experience of being unloved and unlovable because of the loss of significant relationships. This theme of shame has characterized a lot of my own pastoral theology, expressed primarily in two books, *Moving From Shame to Self-Worth* and *Relational Refugees*.

BRIDGING THE GAP BETWEEN THE EIGHTEENTH AND TWENTY-FIRST CENTURIES

The basic argument of this essay is that Wesley's therapeutic understanding of salvation has meaning for the twenty-first-century experience of shame. Wesley's understanding of guilt and forgiveness is relevant for the classical sin experiences of any generation. However, the practice of pastoral theologians, growing out of the twentieth-century cultural experience of shame, calls for a different model of salvation. The argument is that Wesley's significance for the twenty-first century is shown clearly in his healing and therapeutic, practical theological emphasis, as opposed to his juridical or guilt-oriented model.

---

9. Browning, *Thought and Psychologies*, 224.
10. Ibid., 224–25.

Scholars in Wesleyan studies have given warnings about making facile connections between the past and the present. The problem raised has to do with whether Wesley related more to the eighteenth and the modern nineteenth centuries than to the seventeenth.[11] The issues relate to how prominent were the industrial and technological revolutions in Wesley's eighteenth century and whether Wesley's practical theology was modern in the sense of embracing a modern point of view. There is evidence that Wesley was very familiar with the earlier Enlightenment emphasis on the senses as well as the transformation of the economic system that was taking shape because of the industrial and technological revolutions. Yet Wesley's practical theological orientation was fully grounded in his social and cultural location, where guilt psychology, rather than our modern understanding of shame psychology, dominated his thinking. Thus, there is need to update Wesley's practical theology by drawing on his therapeutic and healing model of salvation rather than on his juridical or guilt-oriented model of salvation. Wesley clearly grounded his theology in a guilt orientation where punishment and forgiveness for sin were evident, but he also had a forward-looking, therapeutic view of salvation as capable of healing problems related to personal and interpersonal concerns. The guilt model of salvation kept Wesley clearly grounded in the seventeenth and eighteenth centuries, but the healing and therapeutic model of salvation acknowledged the presence of nineteenth-century concerns.

THE MEANING OF WESLEY'S THERAPEUTIC VIEW OF SALVATION

Jeremy Ayers defines the meaning of Wesley's therapeutic understanding of salvation. Drawing on both Wesley's juridical model of salvation as the forgiveness of guilt and his understanding of salvation as the healing or therapy of the sin-sick soul, Ayers defines exhaustively Wesley's therapeutic meaning of salvation. For him, maturity of faith, which was associated with new birth in the Spirit and in the renewal of the image of God in human beings, was the essence of the therapeutic meaning of salvation.[12] Rooted and grounded in God's love and grace, God seeks, through Jesus Christ, "to revamp the soul deadened by the

---

11. See Gregory, "Long Eighteenth Century," 23. See also Clark, "Changes," 7–10.
12. Ayers, "Wesley's Therapeutic Understanding," 263–97.

world, reviving it to the life in God, facilitated by good works."[13] Ayers describes Wesley's understanding of the therapeutic salvation process as a divine-human interaction, a cooperative process of God-initiated love and responsive human participation, and a divine relationship restores the image of God within human beings. In this Wesleyan understanding of therapeutic salvation, the Holy Spirit plays a vital role, and the restoration of the image of God in human beings is a gift from God. Moreover, in this view of therapeutic salvation, growth and development are processes moving from the healing of the sin-sick soul toward a love of God and one's neighbor.

According to Ayers, Wesley's view of salvation was holistic, and it included the forgiveness of sins as well as the healing of the soul. The guilt model and the therapeutic model worked together in the entire salvation process. Ayers points out, however, that Wesley's eighteenth-century ideas cannot easily be imposed on the twentieth and twenty-first centuries. He says that we live in a world alien to Wesley's. Yet he believes that we can "appropriate his orienting concern and central soteriological aim into pertinent current issues."[14] Thus, the remainder of this essay is an attempt to appropriate for our contemporary lives Wesley's orienting concern.

JOHN WESLEY'S SERMONS

In sermon 89, "The More Excellent Way," Wesley said:

> From long experience and observation I am inclined to think, that whoever finds redemption in the blood of Jesus, whoever is justified, has then the choice of walking in the higher or the lower path. I believe the Holy Spirit at that time sets before him the "more excellent way," and incites him to walk therein; to choose the narrowest path in the narrow way; to aspire after the heights and depths of holiness,—after the entire image of God. But if he does not accept this offer, he insensibly declines into the lower order of Christians.[15]

In the quote above, the statement is made that those who are justified have the choice of walking in a higher or lower path. The reference

---

13. Ibid., 294.
14. Ibid., 295–96.
15. Wesley, *Wesley's Sermons*, 513–14.

Wesley made was to 1 Corinthians 1:31, where those in the church at Corinth were struggling with a falling-back, into cultural forms of self-elevation, by imposing the categories of status and prestige on the expression of spiritual gifts. This reassertion of self-pride following justification caused many in the Corinthian church to fall into what Wesley called "paganism." This was a non-Christian status where persons sought their self-worth by laying their hopes for happiness in the material and secular world. Thus, those who were justified could not move on to sanctification because they were still preoccupied with status concerns. Therefore, Wesley's desire was for those in his reading and listening audience to chose the way of love and not to get hung up on seeking further self-justification and self-validation. Their sliding back into their previous states of worldliness prevented them from moving to the path of greater holiness and happiness in perfecting love, which was the next stage in their spiritual growth.

The problem of moving back into the previous state of seeking self-justification and self-validation through secular, material, worldly means did not only exist during Wesley's time. It is also a problem today. The problem, however, is more insidious in the twenty-first century because of the prevalence of shame rather than guilt. Wesley's juridical model of guilt focused on repentance from one's sin, and the choice one had to make about living one's life was made easier because the relational connections between people were generally solid. The guilt model of sin assumed an intact relational community. The village was very much intact and stable.

The problem in the twenty-first century, however, is that the village is no longer intact, and people cannot make the kinds of choices they need to make because they feel disconnected, unloved, and unlovable. Loss of the village's connections leads to a sense of being unloved. When people feel unloved and unlovable, their ability to make choices is limited. The only real choice for them is confined to the pursuit of a distorted form of love. Normally, this endeavor follows secular or worldly paths, resulting in looking for love in all the wrong places.[16] This worldly path thrusts them into opposition with the path of sanctification.

---

16. *Object relations theory* in the psychoanalytic tradition focuses on the core striving of persons for positive relationships with others. Frustrating relationships with significant others, or the absence of relationships with significant others, can and often will complicate people's ability to make the right choices in their relationships with others.

The critical concern is that this loss of the feeling of being loved, primarily because of the loss of village connections, seriously undermines both the justification and sanctification processes. We become so caught up in the need to be loved that it is hard to let go of the secular paths to happiness and love. Even after the gospel is preached and people find that they are embraced by God, they will fall back into the previous patterns of the world, unless they become connected to a community where they can be loved, embraced, and spiritually mentored.

The critical question for the twenty-first century is, How do the guilt and shame psychological models of today correspond with the eighteenth century's emphasis on guilt? The psychology of shame dominates the present-day understanding of theological anthropology, and the relevant question is, To what extent does Wesley's view of sin have relevance for our contemporary, shame-oriented culture?

Randy Maddox provides some critical insight into the relevance of Wesley's thought for contemporary life and ministry by pointing out that Wesley's theology of salvation integrated the juridical view of guilt with a therapeutic point of view.[17] That is, the juridical emphasis focused on the administration of justice for guilty behavior. Justice focused on God's punishment, the sinner's repentance, and God's forgiveness. The therapeutic view of healing, however, focused on the developmental and therapeutic process of salvation, which rested in finding happiness in God through Jesus Christ. Salvation, then, focused on a relationship with God through a relationship with Jesus Christ, and this relationship embraced healing from guilt as well as healing a broken relationship with God and with other human beings.

The integration of the guilt and therapeutic models of salvation in this relationship helps us to envisage Wesley's relevance for this current century. The concern of the twentieth and twenty-first centuries is shame. The primary feeling that drives human beings today is not the anxiety over guilt or condemnation; it is shame, or the belief and conviction that one is unlovable and will never be loved.[18] The key issue is that

---

See Hunter, ed., *Dictionary*, 796–98.

17. Maddox, *Responsible Grace*, 23.

18. Paul Tillich, in *The Courage To Be*, examines the nature of anxiety in different time periods and how the fear of death changed depending on the cultural and historical time in which people lived. For example, people fear rejection from within or from without because of wrong choices. See *Courage*, 52. Shame is fear and anxiety, but contemporary anxiety is not about being condemned by the wrong choice. Rather,

psychologies of guilt presuppose stable and continuous relational patterns, whereas the psychologies of shame assume the complete breakdown of relational patterns.

Wesley's rhetorical method is grounded primarily in the use of reason to persuade those in his listening and reading audiences about his point of view. One rhetorical method Wesley used was arrangement. He organized a sermon by what has been identified as a motivational sequence. In a motivational sequence, the sermon is organized to maximize the influence on the audience by leading people through a rational process. In this essay, I will use this motivational sequence to examine Wesley's view of juridical guilt as well as his understanding of the therapeutic and healing solution to guilt. To this end, several of Wesley's sermons will be examined. The first is "On Public Diversions"; the second is "On Dress"; the third is "The More Excellent Way"; and the fourth is "On Zeal." The goal of this chapter is to set the stage for updating Wesley's rhetorical method using narrative rhetorical methods.

"ON PUBLIC DIVERSIONS"

The juridical guilt model seems to be illustrated clearly in Wesley's sermon 143 entitled "On Public Diversions."[19] This sermon is based on Amos 3:6. Wesley translates this verse in the following way: "Shall a trumpet be blown in the city, and the people not be afraid? Shall there be evil in the city, and the Lord hath not done it?" In the first sentence of the sermon, he gave the reader and listener serious pause by his attention-getting statement. The statement could have been heard in the following paraphrased language: "You would be better off if you were not concerned by the words of the prophet; for if you were concerned, however, you would be in terror." His attention-getter for his audience was to introduce a note of apprehension about the word the prophet would deliver. After these attention-getting words, Wesley stated the following:

> Are there any men [people] in the world so stupid and senseless, so utterly void of common reason, so careless of their own and their neighbor's safety or destruction, as when an alarm of approaching judgments is given, to show no signs of apprehension?

---

it is the anxiety and threat of the realization that one is not loved and cared for. See Wimberly, *Moving*, 11.

19. Wesley, "On Public Diversions."

> To take no care in order to prevent them, but go on as securely as if no alarm had been given.[20]

He continued, stating that whatever destruction befell them happened because God permitted it and approved it. He said God designed such evil to warn people of a greater evil. How were these rhetorical, attention-getting words taken by the listeners and readers of Wesley's sermon, in his eighteenth-century audience? Making an intelligent guess, I would say that they must have taken the sermon as a judgment for sin and as "fire and brimstone." It must have forced them to await with anxiety the next words that Wesley would say.

I think our contemporary audience would be very critical of Wesley, and would be very disturbed. We would have a great deal of difficulty with the conception of a God that was so judgmental. It is clear to me, however, that Wesley had no difficulty or reservation about introducing a God of judgment who punished human beings for sin. In his notes on the Book of Amos, Wesley pointed out that God reproofs and threatens, but God also promises salvation.[21]

Indeed, Wesley had the attention of those in the audience. What thought-provoking and challenging words were spoken next? He said God's designing of evil was a warning to humankind to avoid God's everlasting vengeance. Wesley conveyed that it was a timely admonition to change one's life.

In the rhetoric of the motivational sequence, Wesley was lifting up the concern for whether his readers and listeners were taking seriously God's warning about God's judgment.

The activities that concerned Wesley included alcohol and gambling. In Wesley's mind, alcohol and gambling were diversions that removed the believer's eyes from God and placed them on the world. Thus, Wesley wanted to introduce the wrath of God as something real for the listener and reader to consider. Yet, at the same time, Wesley pointed out that there was, in relationship with God, a promise of deliverance.

Wesley identified the deadly consequences of these public diversions. Not only would there be God's wrath, there would also be personal, earthly consequences for the person. There would be the consequence of increased covetousness. Covetousness was thought of as soul corrupting,

---

20. Ibid.
21. Wesley, "Wesley's Notes."

and it increased the desire for possessing what others had. In short, public diversions would introduce appetites hard to satisfy.

The deliverance from these deadly consequences was through practice of certain spiritual activities such as participation in Holy Communion, private prayer and devotions, Bible reading, honest work or labor, and public service on behalf of the needy. Of significance was the discipline of living in ways others would find difficult, of walking when one's neighbor would stumble. Practicing mercy to one's neighbor, and especially toward one's afflicted neighbors, was very important. For Wesley, neighbor mercy would lay a good foundation on which to withstand the Day of Judgment.

Wesley addressed this message to the youth, the rich, and the poor. He told the youth to "remember [their] Creator in the days of [their] youth." To the rich, he wrote: "Then you have particular to labour that you may be rich in good works." To the poor, he wrote: "Then you have particular reason to work with your hands that you may provide for your household."

Before leaving Wesley's juridical guilt condemnation model, it is important to explore briefly Wesley's notes on the Book of Amos. These notes provide clues to the connection between this sermon and the sermon on riches explored earlier. Wesley's prophetic voice in "On Public Diversions" addressed something very similar to what he felt about the system of gaining wealth. Public diversions were about laying up treasures on earth.

In Amos 3:6 and related verses, he introduced the multitudes of the poor as persons oppressed and crushed throughout Samaria. He used the words "store up," which referred to laying up treasures that condemned the innocent and took away all of their substance. These words were designed to call people to better accountability for what they did with their money.

In summary, Wesley was deeply committed to the guilt model, or what Randy Maddox called the juridical model of guilt, condemnation, warning, and promise. It is clear that this sermon was judgmental rhetoric, warning people about the consequences of focusing on public diversions like drinking and gambling as sources of human worth. The warning was done in the language of the guilt and condemnation model.

For the twenty-first century, what are the implications of this sermon? The warnings are very instructive for today, since they deal with laying up treasures on earth. Put in another language, the implications of Wesley's warning can be repeated contemporarily. Today's diversions not only include alcohol and gambling addictions; they also include the use of illegal drugs, prescription drugs, food in access, and recreational sex as substitutes for relationships. Diversions make us overly dependent on internet chat rooms and online blogs as places for gratifying the need to be known and famous. In short, a warning about placing one's identity in the hands of the world and its wisdom is clearly a caution that can be laid at our contemporary doorsteps.

From the point of view of updating Wesley's rational rhetoric with narrative rhetoric, the focus would clearly be on the deceptively alluring plot of what public diversions promise. Seeking self-worth and self-validation through physical substances leads to tragic endings. Again the wisdom is clear: attending to the world's promises as ultimate sources of worth produces bondage and has disastrous consequences. Only in relationship with God can one's future be realized. This was Wesley's message, and he used the words of Amos as the warning.

With regard to the implications of narrative rhetoric for living the disciplined life, the key is the need for those seeking their worth in the world to have created for them a safe space where they are able to tell their stories. Moreover, they need caring communities where they can edit their stories in light of the faith stories that connect people with the unfolding, salvational plot of God.

"ON DRESS"

Wesley's "On Dress"—sermon 88—is a continuation of the warning against laying up treasures on earth. Of significance, however, is the fact that he also used the rhetorical wisdom of the pursuit of realistic happiness in this sermon as the method of persuasion rather than the rhetoric of fear and wrath. The rhetoric of happiness fits more with what Maddox says about Wesley's therapeutic emphasis than it does with the juridical guilt emphasis. What makes this sermon different from one using the juridical model is that Wesley's motivational rhetoric lifts up the positive consequences of investing in a relationship with God. In short, the therapeutic rhetorical practices were all about showing people the positive benefits and virtues that come as a result of being in relationship with God. This reflects the pre-Enlightenment focus on the use of doctrine pastorally.

The sermon "The More Excellent Way" also reflects the rhetoric of therapeutic persuasion. This sermon is significant because it assumes that people have the ability to make choices between the worldly path and the spiritual path laid out by God. What is significant is the fact that Wesley and the people in his reading and listening audience could take for granted that they were part of a solid relational community in which they, by and large, felt accepted. It was not the fragilely connected communities of today.

I will return a little later to this discussion of the need to update Wesley's rhetoric of therapy. Presently, I will focus on how Wesley used the rhetoric of therapy to address his audience in the sermon "On Dress."

In "On Dress," Wesley's rhetoric of happiness dominated. The emphasis was not the rhetoric of fear or guilt and condemnation. Rather, the emphasis was to focus the audience on the words of 1 Peter 3:3–4. In these verses, happiness in life was choosing the perfect will of God and not the self-adornment message of the world. He pointed out that the world had its own wisdom and spirit, which conflicted with the will and purposes of God. From the very beginning of the sermon, Wesley was able to capture the attention of the audience through a reasoned argument.

After engaging those in his audience, he introduced the problem with which the audience was struggling. He did this by posing a question, which he thought was on the minds of those in the audience. He said, to paraphrase: I know you have in your minds to ask: "Why concern yourself with preaching about these insignificant and trivial things?" In fact, You say to me, "Why is God so interested in such trivial matters?" He also raised another question to his audience, which, I am sure, would be on the minds of many in this century. He asked, If God created body adornment as good, why talk about it as if it is bad?[22]

Wesley had their full attention as he had asked the real question that needed to be asked. The next step was to tell them why the issue of dress was important for them. Wesley answered these questions. He reasoned that giving themselves completely over to self-adornment made it difficult for them to find happiness in God. The central problem with giving oneself over to self-adornment was pride and thinking of oneself as better than others because of the quality of one's clothing. It was basing self-evaluation and identity on clothing. Wesley wrote:

22. Wesley, "On Dress."

> Nothing is more natural than to think ourselves better because we are dressed in better clothes; and it is scarce possible for a man [person] to wear costly apparel without in some measure, valuing himself upon it.

He continued:

> He could not then but imagine himself to be as much better as he was finer than his neighbor. And how many thousands not only lords and gentlemen, in England, but honest tradesman, argue the same way! inferring the superior value of their persons from the value of their clothes.[23]

Not only was there pride, there was vanity or "the love and desire to be admired and praised." Wesley said, "Aim at pleasing God alone, and all these ornaments will drop off."[24] Focusing on dress also caused anger, because self-adornment produced a disquieted spirit and an inflamed lust. Moreover, getting caught up in dress led to neglect of one's neighbor. He reminded them that God was the source of all resources, and that those in the audience were stewards of such resources.

Wesley continued spelling out the harm of anchoring self-worth on worldly apparel. It damaged the image of God in which human beings were created. It destroyed the image of Christ and inward holiness. It made human beings earthly minded rather than heavenly oriented. Finally, being earthly minded fueled rebellion against God.

Following the introduction of the problem and its elaboration, Wesley moved to the solution to the problem and how this solution needed be visualized. He did not turn to the rhetoric of fear. Rather, he used the therapeutic rhetoric of happiness. He said that God's grace was sufficient to heal these problems.

There are several things to highlight related to the significance of this sermon for the twenty-first century. First, there are implications for the conversation of the honor and shame valuation practices. Earthly conversations about honor placed human worth and value on wealth, power, influence, prestige, and status. To be honorable and worthwhile, one must be identified with what is valued. Shame is defined as not being honorable, because there is the absence of wealth, power, influence, prestige, and status.

---

23. Ibid., no. 9.
24. Ibid., no. 11.

Second, identifying with what the world's wisdom construes as worthwhile entices the person to connect his or her life with tragic plots and outcomes. The tragic outcome is often the lost of real identity and worth. Third, worth and value are related to being connected positively to others, and as a result, respons-ability is fostered. Fourth, happiness is about the care of neighbor and his or her wellbeing.

In the twenty-first century, we cannot assume the solid, communal-based reality that permeated eighteenth-century England and, even, the colonial experiences in North America and on the slave plantations. People in solidly connected communities have the capacity to make what Maddox calls responsible choices in response to God's grace. This is what he means by responsible grace. The emphasis is on respons-ible grace as oppose to respons-able grace.[25] Respons-ible grace assumes the ability to respond where respons-able grace does not assume the ability to respond. Only when people find themselves in a loving and caring community can they be respons-ible. However, those who are linked to fragile communities, where connections hardly exist, find the ability to be respons-able to God's grace very difficult. I will return to this discussion later when I talk about honor and shame culture in twenty-first-century rhetoric. The happiness rhetoric that Wesley assumed is not adequate for this contemporary century.

With regard to the implications of this discussion for upgrading Wesley's rhetoric of reason, the use of narrative rhetoric has the ability to enable those in the audience to examine critically the worldly stories into which they have been led by worldly wisdom. *Narrative rhetorical methods provide protocols, which lead those in the audience to assess the story with which they have identified and how this story has impacted their lives for good or ill.* Narrative rhetorical methods also involve creating relational communities of safe spaces where they can edit the inadequate anchoring of their stories in the honor and shame systems held out by the world. There could also be safe spaces for those in the audience to practice identifying and linking their lives with faith stories and their plots.

---

25. The first time that I heard this distinction between respons-ible grace and respons-able grace was in a summer school class taught by Homer Jernigan in the early 1970's at Boston University.

"THE MORE EXCELLENT WAY"

I will now turn attention to another sermon to illustrate Wesley's therapeutic rhetoric rather than the rhetoric of guilt and condemnation. In the sermon "The More Excellent Way," he used therapeutic rhetoric to urge those in the audience to take the next developmental step in the salvational process, which was sanctification. Developmentally, those in Wesley's audience had already experienced God's justifying grace. Their sins had been forgiven, and their diseased souls had been healed. In justification, the juridical and therapeutic notions are linked. Guilt is forgiven from the juridical view, and the diseased, sin-sick soul is healed from the therapeutic vantage point. The next step in the developmental and therapeutic movement toward happiness is to continue to grow in God's grace and to allow it to carry one to the next level. The next level is sanctification, or perfecting God's love, through the concern for living a holy life and showing love to one's neighbors.

The real danger that Wesley addressed in this sermon was the concern of backsliding, or movement backwards in the therapeutic process of growth in salvation. Wesley used the word *heathen*, which meant non-Christian in the sense of not actively being Christ-centered. Wesley was well aware that the gains in the salvation process could easily be lost if there were no continued practice of spiritual discipline.

Wesley began the sermon by reflecting on 1 Corinthians 12:31. He translated the words to read, "Covet earnestly the best gifts: and yet I show unto you a more excellent way."[26] His initial comment on this passage was to refer to Paul's interpretation of the text to Paul's original audience. Here, Wesley was using rhetorical criticism learned in the university and within the Anglican Church, and he told his audience that Paul wanted his audience to covet or desire earnestly the gifts of the Spirit. Yet, even in desiring spiritual gifts and exercising them, there was a more excellent way. Wesley said that this more excellent way was infallible and would lead to true happiness. Yet, according to Wesley, in earnestly coveting these divine gifts, it was still possible to be miserable in current time as well as in eternal time. Happiness, contrasted with being miserable, had to do, in Wesley's mind, with not only having access to spiritual gifts, but exercising these gifts on the behalf of Christians and non-Christians. In Wesley's rhetorical attention-getting rhetoric,

26. Wesley, *Sermons*, vol. 3.

he alerted his audience to the problem that would occupy the focus of this sermon. That problem was the failure of those in his audience to use the gifts of the Holy Spirit on behalf of those inside and outside the church and Wesleyan societies. This, indeed, was a problem of discipline in the sense of continued practice of the gifts of the Holy Spirit to foster scriptural holiness within the community. The discipline of practicing scriptural holiness referred to those spiritual activities that enabled the practitioner and those being mentored to grow into the image of Christ.

The next rhetorical point in the introduction of the sermon was to connect the disuse of the gifts of the Holy Spirit to the main social problem preventing those in the audience from exercising these gifts. The problem, in Wesley's mind, was the extent to which the church had become socially respectable in the time of Constantine. During the fourth century, the emperor of Rome, Constantine, welcomed all Christians who had been apostates from the faith to return through forgiveness from him. *Apostate*, in this case, refers to the state of denouncing one's faith for the sake of self-interest to prevent being martyred. Despotic emperors prior to Constantine made Christians denounce their allegiance to the Christian church and declare loyalty to the emperor. The end result of the Constantine's forgiveness was a note of social respectability that, in Wesley's mind, made the gifts of the Holy Spirit ineffective. Consequently, his concern was to assure that this did not happen to those in his hearing and reading audience.

What Wesley was addressing in his sermon were the latent results of royal forgiveness that had led to an opportunistic embracing of the honor and shame system of the social evaluation of human worth. To be honorable, people had to identify with what was considered honorable, and this meant wealth, power, prestige, heightened social status, and position. Here again the danger that Wesley addressed in many of his sermons surfaced. This danger was laying up treasures on earth rather than in heaven. Failure to attend to spiritual and heavenly things will cause the gifts of the Holy Spirit to become ineffectual.

The rhetorical problem that Wesley addressed, then, was failure to exercise the gifts of the Holy Spirit because of social respectability. Moreover, Wesley began to move to the next stage of the sermon, which was an exploration of the nature of the problem and how it could be resolved. Here, Wesley addressed the difference between extraordinary gifts and ordinary gifts. Prestige and status would attract people to the extraordinary gifts, and these gifts included the gifts of speaking, persuasion, and so forth. The ordinary gift that all had access was the way of love. This was the more excellent way.

"ON ZEAL"

To this point, three models of Wesley's approach to sin have been explored. The first model was the juridical view of sin, where the motivating factor for change was the fear of condemnation. The second view of sin was a therapeutic view of sin, and the motivating factor leading to God was cure of the sin-sick soul. Here the emphasis was on finding happiness in God as the prime motivation for life. These two models focused on the theme of justification by grace through faith, and people were made right with God due either to fear or to the desire for happiness. The third model was a continuation of the theme of happiness in God, but the difference was in the fear of falling back into a prejustifying state if one did not grow. The shift in emphasis was on the need to continue to grow, and the motivation was to continue to grow in grace for fear of regressing to the former state. In short, the third model moved from justification to the stage of sanctification, and growth in grace toward perfection. Wesley's fourth model was a continuation of the theme of growing toward perfection, with the motivation shifting, in the sermon "On Zeal," to carefully attend to those deceptions that threaten to prevent further growth in the sanctification process.[27] This fourth model emphasized a narrative understanding of sanctification rather than a therapeutic understanding of sanctification. A narrative view of sanctification focused on growing toward perfection, but not for fear of falling back or losing ground. Rather, the focus was on the desire to grow more toward Christlikeness. The emphasis shifted away from fear of loss to the rewards of being Christlike and responding in faith in service to others. In other words, growing in perfecting love became the chief end, and happiness came in knowing one was being faithful to God and executing responsible grace. There was a nuanced shift in emphasis toward the positive benefits resulting from a relationship with divinity and not the negative fear of loss.

The sermon "On Zeal" represents nuanced emphasis, from Wesley's therapeutic model to a narrative emphasis. From Mark Ellingsen's

---

27. Wesley, *Wesley's Sermons*, 465–73.

understanding of Wesley's thinking, narrative is the process of movement toward renewing creation and the self through the deification process.[28] It was the ever-growing discipline of becoming like God. It was Christlikeness, and Jesus was the second Adam, who redeemed creation through his incarnation. Thus, narrative theology was the movement toward becoming Christlike. The sermon "On Zeal" revealed how this process of deification worked.

The rhetoric in the sermon "On Zeal" began with the following statement: "There are few subjects in the whole compass of religion that are of greater importance than this. For without zeal it is impossible, either to make any considerable progress in religion whether in temporal or spiritual things."[29] Immediately following this statement, Wesley mentioned emphatically that some dynamic capacity was needed to prevent remaining in the same place. Here, Wesley emphasized that faith required movement and growth in service to one's neighbor both temporally and spiritually. Yet, he further pointed out that the zeal must be of the right kind.

He pointed out that it was possible to distinguish between good zeal and bad zeal because of the deceitfulness of the human heart.[30] Human passions have the capacity to be self-justifying, and Wesley felt that very little attention had been given to how to discern between good and bad zeal. Rhetorically, therefore, his task in the sermon was to convince those in his reading and listening audience to differentiate Christian zeal from counterfeit zeal. Obviously Wesley felt urgency to address this important problem because it was central to his notion of growth and development in salvation, namely through sanctification, or growing toward perfection.

Following the rhetoric of the motivational sequence, Wesley sought to address the problem of distinguishing good and bad zeal by making three points. He sought to describe the nature of Christian zeal, to delineate its properties, and to help his audience visualize the practical implications of his analysis.

He began by defining the meaning of zeal in the Greek language, found in Galatians 4:18. He pointed out that Christian zeal was the

---

28. Ellingsen, *Reclaiming*, 71.
29. Wesley, *Wesley's Sermons*, 465.
30. Ibid., 466.

passion or desire on behalf of a religious object or end.[31] What made zeal religious was charity or love, according to Wesley. Love was the chief ingredient in Christian zeal. It was the love of God and the love of neighbor. It followed that the properties of love were the properties of zeal.

The rhetoric of persuading through emphasis on reward rather than on fear pointed to pre-Enlightenment influence on Wesley's thought. First, being in relationship with God, in pre-Enlightenment thought, emphasized the benefits of such a relationship, and the benefits were not only happiness. They also were the development of religious virtues and characteristics.[32] The emphasis was on human flourishing as the result of being in relationship with God, and this flourishing had everything to do with translating this flourishing into one's relationship to one's neighbor. The qualities that benefited neighborliness included humility, meekness, patience, and giving the self over to divine providence, or, in Wesley's thought, trusting God, knowing that everything would work out fine in one's love of neighbor.

Flourishing in personal growth and development was possible because the relationship permeated one's entire soul and holy tempers resulted, according to Wesley's practical theological thought. Holy tempers included long-sufferance, gentleness, meekness, fidelity, temperance, and the mind that was in Christ.[33] God was at the center of the human heart. Works of mercy and works of piety became the activity as a result.

Not only could one see the happiness and flourishing model present in this sermon, it was also possible to envisage the influence of Irenaeus' narrative theological thinking. Ellingsen suggests that it is possible to see clearly Irenaeus' narrative theological influence of eastern Christianity on Wesley's thinking.[34] Narrative meant movement and process. Flourishing, resulting from being in relationship with God, led also to the development of holy tempers and works of mercy and works of piety. Works of mercy included attending to the souls and bodies of others, or to their spiritual and physical needs. Works of piety included

---

31. Ibid., 466–67.
32. Charry, *By the Renewing of Your Minds*, 3.
33. Wesley, *Wesley's Sermons*, 467–68.
34. Ellingsen, *Reclaiming*, 72–73.

"reading and hearing the word, public, family, and private prayers, receiving the Lord's Supper, fasting or abstinence."[35]

The significance of Wesley's connection with Irenaeus and Wesley's understanding of zeal is the relation of narrative rhetoric to the central dynamic of sanctification. Narrative rhetoric not only depicts movement and process; it also highlights the central dynamic of the pull and the drawing power of narrative. The power of Scripture is in its ability to get the hearer or reader to suspend his or her own way of seeing reality and, as the reader or hearer is drawn in, to take on the world as it is revealed in the text.[36] The key is that Scripture draws the reader or hearer into the plot that lies behind the stories and narratives, and this plot is the unfolding of God's rule and reign through the transformation and recreation of the world through Jesus Christ and the call of the church universal. This is not to say that Wesley understood Scripture in this way. It is to say, however, that Wesley understood the dynamic nature of Scripture, and his concept of Scriptural holiness pointed to the dynamic and powerful nature of Scripture. The point is that Wesley did not employ the plot logic of Scripture as the central dynamic of his understanding of the doctrine of sanctification.

Mark Elllingsen, however, points out that in a number of Wesley's sermons he demonstrated that he understood the powerful impact Scripture had on the lives of those who hear biblical stories retold in sermons. Ellingsen points out that in a number of sermons Wesley "identifies his hearers with characters in the biblical accounts."[37] Ellingsen identifies Wesley's sermon "Upon Our Lord's Sermon on the Mount," from 1739, where Wesley likened his readers and hearers to the lives of Pharisees.[38] Indeed, Wesley made the identification for the reader, but the key emphasis made here, however, is on the reader or hearer being drawn into the text through the power of the text itself. The focus of contemporary narrative rhetoric is the power of Scripture, as story, to draw human beings into the dynamic, unfolding plot of God.

---

35. Wesley, *Wesley's Sermons*, 468.

36. The following books help to show the development of a biblical narrative approach, which is the basis of narrative rhetorical criticism: Ellingsen, *Integrity*, 18–52; Goldberg, *Theology and Narrative*; Wimberly, *Using Scripture*.

37. Ellingsen, *Integrity*, 48.

38. Ibid.

WESLEY AND THE TWENTY-FIRST CENTURY

The aim of this chapter has been to explore the significance for the twenty-first century of Wesley's thought about the juridical and therapeutic understanding of salvation. More specifically, the concern was to explore the implications of this model for dealing with the modern experience of shame as the feeling of being disconnected resulting in the feeling of being unloved. Our examination of Wesley's rational rhetorical approach revealed that his thought contained elements of narrative rhetorical criticism. This is especially true regarding process and movement as Wesley tried to draw people into the biblical narrative itself. It was the conclusion, however, that Wesley's narrative orientation was not narrative rhetoric in the sense of emphasizing the power of Scripture to draw hearers and readers into the text and to convince them to adopt plot logic and the world as disclosed by Scripture.[39] While Wesley assumed that the biblical world was different from the secular world, the rhetorical power of the biblical world was assumed, but not part of his actual method of doing practical theology.

Yet, the power of Wesley's thought holds out great promise to speak to contemporary life and, especially, to the problem of shame. Narrative rhetorical methods of persuasion will do three things for Wesley's thought. First, they will bring out the significance of Wesley's understanding of discipline as Scriptural holiness. Second, they will show how narrative rhetoric enhances communal participation and adds to the important notions of recreating Methodist societies and congregations. Finally, they will show how narrative rhetoric speaks to the contemporary problem of human shame.

First, narrative rhetoric will show how being in relationship to God through Jesus Christ and the resultant happiness and the virtues of love of neighbor are not only reinforced by Scripture, but are also nurtured by Scripture. Attending to Scripture as story, and emphasizing its power to draw and to pull persons into God's unfolding plot, supports

---

39. This view of Wesley coincides with what Mark Ellingsen wrote in correspondence with me about Wesley. In this sense, Wesley was not pre-modern. Ellingsen writes, "When I refer to a pre-modern narrative approach, I am thinking in terms of my Yale mentors (Hans Frei, Brevard Childs, and George Lindbeck) who were very Barthian. For them, this approach entails that you begin with the Word of God and lure the hearer/reader into the story. When that happens, the believer's prior experience and questions are overcome/transformed by God's word and the narrative." This correspondence was in an email dated August 31, 2009.

and enhances what God does to the believer in relational discourse. Scriptural holiness becomes development of works of mercy and works of piety resulting from being drawn into God's unfolding salvational plot.

By talking about the power of Scripture to draw human beings into the story and to get them to suspend their customary ways of seeing reality, the emphasis is on a pre-modern understanding of the power of Scripture. According to Ellingsen, the absence of this sense of the power of Scripture in Wesley made Wesley modern rather than pre-modern. Therefore, the suggestion of this author is that Wesley's use for today is in recovering more fully the pre-modern sense of Scripture.[40]

Second, narrative rhetoric by its very nature is communal. Narrative rhetoric assumes that Scripture itself is a living community of persons, with God encountering a living community of persons. Scripture is communion with the saints and God. The power of narrative is that it requires storytellers and story-listeners. This was the significance of the Wesleyan societies wherein people could find a safe space for their stories to unfold and wherein all involved could see God's work at the center of their lives. Wesley's original vision of a small, nurturing society needs to be enhanced by an understanding of the drawing power of Scripture as well as by the small community of mutual interpreters of what God is doing to sustain the sanctification process.

Narrative rhetoric also helps those within the societies to envisage the interconnection between justification and sanctification. There are other interconnections, including the personal and communal, practices of personal piety and practices of mercy to others, and the interconnections of the individual and communal lives of persons in these societies.

Finally, narrative rhetoric through biblical storytelling and story-listening in the daily lives of those societies, helps to respond to the shame that characterizes modern experience. Pastoral counseling and psychology reveal that people who are disconnected are looking for a safe place to tell their stories. The narrative rhetorical model embraces the psychological model of shame, which relates to the person's need for love rather than to his or her guilt. Rhetorical narrative does not neglect guilt. Rather, it recognizes that addressing guilt first often blocks the natural emergence of guilt once people feel loved and cared for. Pastoral counseling and pastoral psychology reveal that people are freed

40. Ellingsen, *Integrity*, 48.

up to discuss their self-sabotaging behavior when they genuinely feel embraced and loved by others.

Before this chapter concludes, Glenn Henderson must be re-introduced, especially with regard to the narrative model updating Glenn's own life. Glenn's transformation was clearly a process where God's love for him and his wife became evident. Moreover, God brought healing to his wife, and Scripture played a major role. Each chapter began with a scriptural quote, and he would always work Scripture into the telling of his story. In fact, his entire book is a narrative account of God's significant participation in his life, and he learned to tell his story using God's story as the background and foreground.

Indeed, updating of Wesley's rhetoric of reason with narrative rhetoric holds out a great deal of promise for making his thinking relevant for the twenty-first century. It is the next task of this work to address Wesley's public theology, or his attempt to address public issues through his treatises.

Chapter 3

God's Present But Not Yet Future

This chapter is about the big picture or the biggest frame that gives the best understanding of Wesley's theology. The big picture is often called God's ultimate goal for creation including human beings, and this big picture is often called the reign of God. The reign of God is often explained as God's participation in history, establishing God's own story and how human beings are called on to participate in what God is doing. In fact, some have indicated that God's rule and reign is God's story or external history.[1] God's story and God's history is what makes human beings' stories meaningful, and when God's story, or the big story, impacts our individual and our church stories, our lives become meaningful. It is God's big story and God's ultimate goal for participating in history that gives God's work and our calling to vocation meaning.

I have discussed Wesley's pre-Enlightenment emphasis on happiness and virtue, beginning first with being in relationship with God. This originating love relationship manifested itself in the love of God, neighbor, and self in Wesley's thought. In the previous chapter, we talked about Wesley's orientation to salvation as healing and therapeutic. Yet, this healing and therapeutic point of reference cannot be understood fully without it being situated in a much larger theological frame: the larger frame called orthonarrative or right story.[2] It is contextualizing Wesley's orthodoxy, his healing and therapeutic, salvational theology within a larger narrative framework, that gives Wesley's thought significance for the twenty-first century.

---

1. Neibuhr, *Meaning*, 59–66.
2. Runyon, "Orthopathy," 296.

This chapter, then, is about what is called reframing. Reframing is not reinventing Wesley's practical theology for it to have contemporary relevance. It is not remaking the traditional thought of the past for the purposes of developing new perspectives and practices while building on the past in light of God's Spirit, as suggested in the thinking of Mary Elizabeth Mullino Moore in her article "The United Methodist Church at 40: What Can We Hope For?"[3] I speak of reframing as the process of rediscovering previous theological insights, which were present in Wesley's thought, but which need to be retrieved for their contemporary relevance. At present, it is important to examine Wesley's thought in light of a narrative rhetorical frame, and the intent of such rhetorical assessment is to discern how Wesley sought to convince those in his reading and listening audiences to identify with God's unfolding plot of salvation, which provided the ultimate direction human beings were to take in their pilgrimage on earth. My thesis is that Wesley's narrative rhetoric was grounded in a story of a hopeful vision of God's future defined as an "already but not yet eschatology."[4]

The basic theme of this chapter is that Wesley's rhetoric was grounded in a narrative vision of the future that contrasted God's present and future with the prevailing cultural stories, beliefs, and convictions present in his day. Throughout Wesley's practical theology, it is possible to envisage his method of critical thinking, which compared his theology with the prevailing cultural stories existing in the public square and common marketplace. His rhetoric was anchored in his awareness that the cultural vision of the prevailing economic and social situation was very limited and that their plots led to tragic ends when viewed in light of what God was doing when God was working out God's eschatological future.

The major aims of this chapter are several. First, I will examine Wesley's narrative rhetoric, which contrasted the unfolding story of God's plot for the future with the prevailing vision and plots of his day. I will use one sermon entitled "A More Excellent Way" to demonstrate how he skillfully used narrative rhetoric to lead people to re-author and re-edit their own personal beliefs and convictions in light of God's unfolding future. Second, I will explore Wesley's metaphorical use of images as his rhetorical strategy for drawing people into God's eschatological

---

3. Moore, "Church at 40," 69–71.
4. Wimberly, "Wesley and the Twenty-first Century," 93.

future. The treatise "An Earnest Appeal to Men of Reason and Religion" will be the focus of this discussion. Finally, I will draw out implications of this analysis for our life in the twenty-first century. Before turning to Wesley's thought and its implications for our contemporary lives, I return to the case of Glenn Henderson.

GLENN HENDERSON AND GOD'S PLAN

In his chapter entitled "The Plan of Amazing Grace," he drew on Jeremiah 29:11 to place his transformative conversion experience with God in its larger narrative frame. He quoted all of Jeremiah 29:4–14, but it is verse 29:11 that gives the big-picture meaning of Glenn's newfound experience. "For I know the plans I have for you, 'declares the Lord,' plans to prosper you and not to harm you, plans to give you hope and a future."[5] Glenn and his wife indicated their "focus was on what [they] wanted for [themselves] and what [they] wanted God to do in response."[6] They could care less what plans God had for their lives. From the moment of their awareness of their short-sightedness, they began to surrender fully to God, which meant that "God's agenda" was to transform their lives for God's sanctifying plan for using their business toward God's establishing God's rule and reign on earth. Thus, God set Glen and his wife on a salvational and healing process that included not only entering them in right relationship with God, but they also began discipleship training in God's perfection of holiness in their lives and in their business practices.

A MORE EXCELLENT WAY

In Wesley's credo, expressed in his treatise "The Character of a Methodist," he set forth his beliefs and convictions, which informed his narrative rhetoric. He wrote:

"Blessed be the God and Father of our Lord Jesus Christ, who according to his abundant mercy, hath begotten me again to a living hope—of an inheritance incorruptible, undefiled, and that fadeth not away, reserved in heaven for me!"[7] This passage of Scripture referred to 1 Peter 1:3, and Wesley said this passage related to the regeneration of

---

5. Henderson, *Treasures*, 152.
6. Ibid., 159.
7. Wesley, *Works*, 342.

persons to a living hope. This meant a spiritual renewal, which revived the heart and made the soul alive and prosperous.[8]

To Wesley, the starting point for true happiness was the person's relationship with God through Jesus Christ, and following this, the soul was made alive and vigorous through the Holy Spirit, which suggested a movement toward sanctification, or continued growth in love.

Building on Wesley's starting point for his practical theology of happiness, in which happiness rested in a human being's relationship with God, I shift now to his sermon entitled "The More Excellent Way." In this sermon, Wesley came the closest to articulating his vision of a narrative rhetoric, which contrasted two story plots. One story plot represented a tragic vision of reality, which was detrimental to the human soul on the one hand. On the other hand, there was another plot whose end was hopeful, and this plot would lead ultimately to happiness on earth and in heaven.

The best approach to explicating Wesley's narrative rhetoric is to examine his use of the financial metaphor of "laying up." This is a metaphor Wesley used to explain his understanding of both the danger of riches and the rewards of being in relationship with God and God's unfolding rule and reign. Wesley made an analogy about investing in the banks of this world, or the "earthly bank," or in the coming rule and reign of God, or the heavenly bank. In "The More Excellent Way," he wrote rhetorically, with the intention of persuading those in his audience of the following:

> But suppose it were not forbidden, how can you on principles of reason, spend your money in a way which God may possibly forgive, instead of spending it in a manner which he will certainly reward? You will have no reward in heaven for what you lay up; you will, for what you lay out. Every pound you put into the earthly bank is sunk: it brings no interest above. But every pound you give to the poor is into the bank of heaven. And it will bring glorious interest; yea, and, as such, will be accumulating to all eternity.[9]

The key point is that Wesley identified two stories or narrative plots, and each had its own conclusion or plot ending. The plot ending was different for each story. Investing in the earthly bank ended in a

---

8. Wesley, "Notes."
9. Wesley, "Way," 4:5.

tragic conclusion. It had a limited *telos*, or end. Investing in the heavenly bank had the end of investing in God's future, since God's future involved God's rule and reign, and certainly, God's rule and reign had a lot to do with love relationships among people and God. Investing in the earthly realm solely led to bankruptcy with no interest in the future. Earthly investing flirted with disaster and deficits in meaningful living.

Wesley also used the metaphor "Spirit of Christ" in opposition to the image of "spirit of the world" to define the more excellent way. The characteristic marks of the Spirit of Christ within the lives of believers were complete trust in God and believing that the aim of God's call was to please God.[10] One was not to aim toward laboring for that which was perishable, but one was to aim for that which would endure. One was able to stay focused by developing the virtues of holiness, which included love of neighbor, the practice of prayer, and gestures of self-sacrifice. Avoid settling for ease, pleasure, or riches, but aim for pleasing God. An important practice was returning thanks for what God had provided to eat, recognizing that God provided for human sustenance. Human conversation should be harmless, and there should be no carrying of tales, backbiting, or speaking evil of others. Conversations with others should edify, nurture, and build them up.

In addition to these helpful behavioral tasks was the reminder that rest and relaxation were important dimensions for self-care. Moreover, one's choice of diversions also had to be carefully made with holiness in mind. Sports, hunting, shooting, fishing, and all other kinds of healthy activities were important and could involve both sexes. Theatrical plays, attending concerts, lectures, and the like were dimensions of self-care through holiness. Reading was also considered to be important, but the choice of diversion could be noble or ignoble. Wesley was displeased with cockfighting along with gambling and inflicting cruelty to animals. Things that got in the way of holiness included profane values and debauchery. The point was that Wesley believed that all behavior, including diversions, should be in love and fear of God.[11] He also included cultivating and improving land as an important diversion, and visiting the sick, homeless, and parentless as important practices in which to invest time.

---

10. Ibid., 3:3.
11. Ibid., 5:4.

The point is that Wesley's narrative rhetoric focused on convincing people that trusting God to work out providentially God's plot within the world led to happiness and virtue. Trusting and investing in the plot of the world would lead to destruction and loss of happiness. Theological providence informs Wesley's conviction that it was possible for God to generate positive outcomes from negative situations.

Indeed, Wesley used a number of rhetorical strategies to persuade people to choose the plot that led to eternal happiness in this world and in the world coming. First, common images and metaphors were used to capture people's imagination. Images such as those of investment banking drawn from the emerging, capitalistic, eighteenth-century banking system were good examples. His contrasting the two different ends of the story plots, of investing in this world or in the world that was coming, was another example. One form of investing led to the loss of vitality in life and to destruction, while the other form led to ultimate happiness.

Wesley also used the analogy between long-term investment strategies to highlight the significance of postponing immediate gratification. Sacrificing immediate short-term gains for long-term happiness was a very effective argument. This was the most reasonable strategy, in Wesley's mind.

Wesley also rhetorically appealed to his audience's sense of early church history for drawing contrasting analogies related to what he called vain imagination. The Emperor Constantine manipulated early Christians to trust in the abilities of the government to generate happiness, rather than investing in God's call to invest in the coming of God's present but not yet rule and reign. Wesley called Constantine's rule the fatal period. In fact, he said that the gifts of the Holy Spirit almost totally ceased during his rule.[12] He called this period of time a miserable mistake. He used the metaphoric term "waxed cold" to refer to the loss of the "Spirit of Christ." People no longer saw evidence of God's movement in the church through the signs and wonders and miracles of the extraordinary gifts of the Holy Spirit.

To further make his case for seeking happiness in God's future instead of in what this world had to offer, he began to delineate the gifts of the Holy Spirit. He pointed out that even the genuine gifts of the Holy Spirit could be corrupted by the spirit of this world.[13] Gifts of convincing

12. Ibid., 2.
13. Ibid., 3.

speech, of persuasion, of knowledge, and the gift of faith could be corrupted if practiced without the gift of love. Drawing on Constantine's example, Wesley warned that the gifts of the Spirit could be used in the service of other goals than those of God's rule and reign.

Wesley then shifted his attention to the actual intent of his sermon, which I label as his *narrative intent*. He held out to his audience the distinction between those who walked by faithful practices toward the goal of attaining the "mind of Christ."[14] He used the metaphor of walking as the journey toward Christian perfection. It is in Wesley's notion of Christian perfection that I understand his narrative intent. In developing a mind of Christ, Christians were called to embrace and imitate Jesus Christ and his mission as well as to invest themselves in the unfolding and coming rule and reign of God. They were to allow themselves to be led by the Holy Spirit's trustworthy, infallible guidance as they participated in God's unfolding story of salvation. *Infallible*, here, does not mean inerrancy in light of every word in Scripture being true. Rather, Wesley's notion of infallibility had to do with trusting in God's providential participation in carrying out the ends of God's rule and reign.

Another rhetorical strategy Wesley used to entice people into "the more excellent way" was his emphasis on the role of the Holy Spirit. He was convinced that human beings did not have the innate capacity to will, through their own efforts, to choose the more excellent way. He believed the Holy Spirit incited human beings to choose the more excellent way and "to aspire after the heights and depths of holiness—after the entire image of God."[15] There was, indeed, an underlying problem in human beings if they trusted only in themselves and their own abilities to choose the right path. He believed that outside a relationship with God human beings would choose a lesser road to travel. Human beings needed the guidance of the Holy Spirit to make the right choices.

Another narrative rhetorical strategy used by Wesley was his effort to get people to invest their lives in their eschatological vocation. Wesley believed that the Holy Spirit also led people into the "business of their calling."[16] He sought to show people that the Holy Spirit could be trusted to lead them toward labor and work that pleased God and produced satisfying and meaningful results that would be long-lasting and would

14. Ibid., 5.
15. Wesley, "Way," 6.
16. Ibid., 3:1.

not perish. This calling would also produce happiness that would endure and eventuate in everlasting life.

Wesley's understanding of the contrast between investing in this life and investing in the coming but not yet world that God inaugurated in Jesus Christ has profound implications for our own ability to think critically about what is going on in our lives in the twenty-first century. Wesley understood what today we call status anxiety. He understood that people's concern for their own economic wellbeing had little to do with the basic need for the provision of food, shelter, and sustenance in life. Rather, he understood that one of the basic efforts of human beings was to secure their ultimate happiness and security, and the philosophy of human beings has been to seek to gain these important ends of happiness and security through the pursuit of economic and social prestige and status, and through gaining power, wealth, and identity. Moreover, he understood that worldly investment usually meant that achieving these ends came at the expense of others and blocked the needed manifestation of love. In short, Wesley understood what today we call status anxiety. That is, he understood that seeking this world for human worth and dignity as well as happiness would lead to status anxiety or the fear that the loss of these things would mean ultimate damnation and destruction. In more conclusive words, Wesley understood that human beings had vain imaginations, and this vanity reinforced sin and their desire to seek in this world their self worth and dignity. The end result of this vain striving usually was cost to others and faulty reasoning.

Of significance also was Wesley's effort not only to enable people to develop critical thinking about the prevailing beliefs and convictions about investing in worldly wealth, status, and prestige, but also to help people to develop the ability "to edit" and to "re-author" their internal and distorted beliefs about their status and investment in this world. Editing and re-authoring are narrative strategies used by family therapists to reorient people's lives toward more growth-producing practices.[17] For Wesley, the Holy Spirit was the infallible or reliable and trustworthy guide for enabling people to disconnect from enticements to anchor and invest their lives in this world and its images of happiness. He kept emphasizing that human beings alone did not have the capacity to make the investment in God's call to vocation. He said that for human beings this was impossible. "But all things are possible with God," and by

---

17. See White, *Re-Authoring Lives*; and Wimberly, *Recalling*.

God's grace, it was possible.[18] He urged people to do what they could do, and this was to continue in prayer. Prayer opened up new possibilities to edit, re-author, and revise people's beliefs and convictions that were limited to this world. It was through the investment in prayer that people could disconnect from investing in this world their hope for happiness.

> In like manner you may suit your devotions to your inward state, the present state of your mind. Is your soul in heaviness, either from a sense of sin, or through manifold temptations? Then let your prayer consist of such confessions, petitions, and supplications as are agreeable to your distressed situation of mind. On the contrary, is your soul in peace? Are you rejoicing in God? Are his consolations not small with you? Then say, with the Psalmist, "Thou art my God, and I will love thee: Thou art my God, and I will praise thee.[19]

Wesley concludes this line of exhortation by affirming that from this reasoning they must surely see clearly the more excellent way.

He also believed that surrendering people's will to God's will would enable them to divert their lives from seeking worldly pleasures and to invest in God's future. In short, trusting the Holy Spirit as a guide led human beings to the more excellent way.

NARRATIVE RHETORIC IN "EARNEST APPEAL TO MEN OF REASON AND RELIGION"

In Wesley's "Earnest Appeal to Men of Reason and Religion," he used a metaphor that captured what I believe was one of his best examples of narrative rhetoric. I refer to narrative rhetoric as his attempt to convince his audience that there was another level of reality that existed beyond this current world of existence. This world was an alternative to his contemporary world's story of what was real.

In "Earnest Appeal," he used the metaphor "palate of the soul." He described the meaning of this metaphor using analogous images related the human appetite. He said: "It is (if I may be allowed the expression) the palate of the soul; for hereby a believer 'tastes the good word, and the

---

18. Wesley, "Way," 1:1.
19. Ibid., 2:1.

powers of the world to come;' and 'hereby he both tastes and sees that God is gracious,' yea, 'and merciful to him a sinner.'"[20]

Of significance is Wesley's reliance on the Pauline vision of the present but not yet vision of the coming of God's rule on earth, which is present in part, but its final completion will come at the end of time. For example, in "The More Excellent Way," he commented on 1 Corinthians 12:31, which reads, "Covet earnestly the best gifts: and yet I show unto you a more excellent way."[21] Wesley believed, along with the Pauline vision, that all of the promises of God, including happiness and virtue in this world and in the world to come, were grounded in the coming world of reality that was present "now" but whose completion would come later. He believed that this real world was invisible, but it was a system of things eternal.[22] This system was the basis of the love of God shed abroad in a believer's heart. Faith in this coming world of reality is what saved the Christian from an "uneasy mind," from "the inexpressible listlessness and weariness" within the world and within our own lives, and it is what causes Christians not to be fooled by this world's enticements to lay up treasures on earth or to invest in a corrupt bank rather than in an non-corrupt reality.[23] This world to come was accessed through the power of the Holy Spirit, and the evidence of the presence of this invisible world was love. There was in this invisible world "supernatural evidence," and this evidence was discernable through the Spirit.[24] The evidence abounded in Scripture, and this would be discerned only through the "eyes of faith" and not by "eyes of the flesh." Wesley believed that participating in the present but not yet future was the source of all happiness as well as the power to live the new life in the Spirit. It empowered sanctification and the ability to live the new life.

In "Earnest Appeal," Wesley asked why human beings did not have this vision of faith to discern this invisible world? In his characteristic rhetorical question-and-answer style, he answered: "It is the gift of God."[25] It was something that human beings could not create through reason and was beyond the power of human beings to create themselves.

20. Wesley, *Works*, 4.
21. Wesley, "Way," 1.
22. Wesley, *Works*, 5.
23. Ibid.
24. Ibid., 4.
25. Ibid., 5.

Knowledge of such a world was available to all, but it was a gift that came from beyond the human self.

Wesley argued with the contemporary narrative or story of his time, which grounded itself in the trust of human reason, created by the Enlightenment distrust of divine revelation. Moreover, Wesley used his rhetorical style of questioning and answering to contrast his own understanding of the relationship of revelation and reason. For example, Wesley asked in "Earnest Appeal": "Can you give yourself faith? Is it now in your power to see, or hear, or taste God? Have you already, or can you raise in yourself, any perception of God, or of an invisible world?"[26] Wesley answered: "You not only do not, but cannot, by your own strength, thus believe. The more you labour so to do, the more you will be convinced 'it is the gift of God.'"[27] Wesley said it was the free gift of God, not because of human merit, worthiness, or holy behavior. It was available to the holy and the unholy. It was viewed as a gift offered to those whose lives were headed for destruction, but who at the last moment asked God to be merciful on themselves as sinners.[28]

What is clear to me is that Wesley fully believed he was teaching. He felt that one could not understand why people of reason would turn against what he had been teaching. This was beyond his capacity to conceive.

Wesley also believed that love of God and love of neighbor were grounded fundamentally in this invisible world to come, yet were available in the present primarily though the power of the Holy Spirit. Of course, Wesley assumed that all human beings could experience God in the way he experienced God: in a very personal way. He could not understand why people could not embrace a God who could be experienced as love, unless the reason of these people got in the way.

Of course, today we have deeper knowledge about how our experiences as human beings, and the quality of our living experiences, in the world of pain, suffering, oppression, injustice, and in the absence of love, could block or hinder our experience of God's love in our lives. Of course, Wesley believed that God's love could breakdown any barriers to God's love, but my own experience working in pastoral counseling has convinced me that, for some, the level of reasoning that Wesley expected

---

26. Ibid.
27. Ibid., 6.
28. Ibid.

cannot happen. Our inhumanity to each other can block our level of reasoning, yet, through God's Spirit, it is clear to me that God is at work, in the depth of the human consciousness, seeking to break through the hold that our inhumanity has on others.

The point, however, is that Wesley's practical theological conviction was that human beings could experience God's love and grace in their lives, no matter their status in life. I fundamentally believe this, yet my experience working with people who have suffered abuse and were recruited, by others, to serve the needs of others shows how such abuse often stands in the way of their ability to discern the work of God in the depths of their lives. On the other hand, I am convinced that God does provide people whose lives have been healed from abuse to lead people who have been similarly abused to envisage the love of God at work in their lives. This is why Wesley's emphasis on the small group and class system is so appropriate for the twenty-first century. The work of God through the Holy Spirit mediates the transforming love of God.

In summary, Wesley believed in two different stories. They had two different plots. One was oriented to this world, and commitment to this world led to human destruction and unhappiness. The story of the present but not yet completed rule and reign of God was the real, true world. Commitment to it brought happiness in this perishable and corruptible world as well as in the world to be completed.

WESLEY AND THE TWENTY-FIRST CENTURY

Wesley's question-and-answer rhetorical style in "Earnest Appeal" focused on the role of reason in faith and why it was not possible for all people to envisage God in the way Wesley himself was able to experience God. In my mind, it was because there were two opposing narratives or stories prevalent with two opposing plots. Therefore, Wesley believed that allegiance to one story led to happiness and virtue while allegiance to the other did not.

In Wesley's mind, these two stories were based on Wesley's beliefs about the way human beings came to know or derived knowledge. More precisely, the issue had to do with whether the source of knowledge came from within the person or the self, on the one hand, or whether it came from outside the self, on the other hand. Or, to put this issue of knowledge in Wesleyan terms, the concern was whether the source of human knowledge of God and the world came from God or from within the self. Of course, some would say that this question is a false concern since, ultimately, God is the source of all knowledge, and the capacity to achieve knowledge through human reason was part of creation. Thus, there is no real dichotomy between natural knowledge emerging from within persons and revealed knowledge that comes from God. For Wesleyans, this concern for natural theology is a fundamental problem for the twenty-first century.

Theodore Runyon brings contemporary clarity to this issue for the twenty-first century about the origin of religious experience and its source. He says:

> First, in order to be "right" it must have a source in God, it must transcend subjectivism. As Jurgen Moltman has said, "the modern concept of experience . . . threatens to transform experience into the experience of the self. Nineteenth-century Romanticism and Pietism tended to reduce experience to feelings within the individual. Only you can feel the way you do, and therefore experience was reduced to the gut level of the individual. If with Wesley we go behind this nineteenth-century approach back to the eighteenth century, and to the empirical method proposed by Locke, we see that the structure of Lockean epistemology avoided this subjectivism because in the knowing process it gives priority to the world external to the self to disclose itself through evidence registering upon the senses.[29]

Runyon points out that both Wesley and Locke rejected Cartesianism, which was the source of Enlightenment thinking. Cartesianism rejected the notion that knowledge of God had its source outside of the person. Wesley believed that true knowledge of God came as the result of God's self-disclosure through the Holy Spirit.[30] It came from beyond the self; therefore, the notion of privatism of knowledge of God was an error.

For Runyon, transcendental subjectivism was the philosophical basis for Wesley's notion of right feeling or orthopathy. Not only was transcendental subjectivism a mark or characteristic of orthopathy, it was also a characteristic of Wesley's orthonarrative, given my own assessment of Wesley's thought in the previous section of this chapter. Wesley's orthonarrative placed emphasis on the "right plot," or the right *telos* or

---

29. Runyon, "Orthopathy," 296.
30. Ibid.

direction of the story, and his view was grounded in God's current but not yet rule and reign. It was God's unfolding story of the redemption of creation, and its origination was from God's own self-disclosure in Jesus Christ. Thus, the source of the story was God's incarnation in human history, but this story is ongoing and will be completed at the end of time. Thus, the incarnation is the source of the idea that knowledge came from outside of the created order. Thus there are two distinct realities existing simultaneously.

I concur with Runyon that Wesley's orthodoxy or right doctrine, his orthopraxy or right practice, and his orthopathy or right feeling rested in the eighteenth-century empirical approach, which was influenced by Locke. Locke's eighteenth-century empirical approach rested in the conviction that knowledge of God was beyond the self.[31] Thus, orthonarrative established its vision of human hope on the basis of the unfolding of God's present and not yet rule and reign.

It is crucial to recognize that the issue that tended to contrast knowledge of God, as well as hope in the self and human feelings rather than in God's unfolding story of salvation, redemption, and reign, is a twenty-first-century issue that can be envisaged in the present day problems identified in the beginning of this book. These problems are status anxiety and the narcissism epidemic. Status anxiety "is the fear that one will be stripped of dignity and worth if one does not have the material wealth to be recognized."[32]

Status anxiety is the belief and conviction that one's worth and value are defined from within the current culture rather than from the emerging presence of God and the establishing of God's present but not yet rule. It is seeking self-validation within one's own acquisition of upward economic, social, political, and status movement in society. The end result is that worth and dignity are lodged in the self's ability to achieve social status, but the fallacy of this locating of dignity in the self's achievement in society was what Wesley called "laying up treasures on earth" rather than investing in God's future. Tragic consequences result, as in the case of our current worldwide financial and economic crises.

Akin to status anxiety is the phenomenon called the "narcissism epidemic." Contemporary narcissism is a deterioration of the pursuit of self-worth and dignity to a form of self-centeredness and self-admiration

---

31. Ibid.
32. Wimberly, "Wesley and the Twenty-first Century," 98.

grounded in technology and the disconnection of people from human community. I describe it in the following way:

> Thus, the major emphasis is on being wealthy or famous or popular without having any real legacy of achievement or backing. Even the pursuit of fame through infamy and anti-social behavior aided by the Internet is rampant. Among other practices, maxing out credit loans that one cannot afford just to appear successful, indeed, was the straw that broke the back of our economy.[33]

My critique is essentially the same critique provided by Runyon concerning nineteenth-century Romanticism and Pietism. The self cannot be the source of human happiness and virtue. The self can be a recipient of the kinds of relationships that come from God's self-disclosure through the Holy Spirit and manifested in human relationships. Moreover, human dignity and worth are gifts from God and are not generated from within the human soul or self. Nor are human worth and dignity established through the pursuit of social and cultural status. Thus, this notion of seeking ultimate worth and value through social achievement and cultural admiration leads to tragic outcomes. They do not save. Only being anchored in God's unfolding story of reality will lead to happiness and virtue.

Another dimension of orthonarrative is transformation understood in the light of participaton in God's unfolding plot of salvational history. In the H. Richard Niebuhr sense, we are transformed when our personal stories are connected to God's unfolding story of God's establishing God's reign.[34] It is when our inner histories encounter God's outer or external history unfolding in our lives that we confront the generative source of all human transformation. Thus, transformation is a process of surrendering to a source of happiness and virtue that has its origin outside of the self. In reality, when we connect our stories with God's story, we surrender our own tragic plot, or we update our stories in such a way that they are consistent with God's salvational outcome. Therefore, happiness and virtue are encountered in the midst of our narcissistic pursuits, and we find our ultimate source of our pursuits for happiness and virtue in God.

---

33. Ibid., 99.
34. Niebuhr, *Meaning*.

In addition to orthonarrative being transformative, it is active through our participation in community. Wesley believed that character formation and transformation were nurtured with community. The very nature of grace, in his thinking, was the fact that God's goodness had to be shared. Grace is nurtured within human discourse, interaction, and conversation.[35] The sources of grace mediated within the church—such as participation in worship, the taking of the sacrament, and communal prayer—are essential practices for the transformation of our proclivity to anchor our lives in our narcissistic pursuits. In short, orthonarrative practices are communal.

Closely related to the communal nature of orthonarrative is the conclusion that it is rational. Rationality in Wesley's thought was clearly about interpretation, reflection, and attribution, in that the goal was to derive meaning or give meaning to what we experience. According to Runyon, reason, in Wesley's thought, was essentially to keep in check the "irrational excesses of enthusiasm of which the Wesleyan movement was often accused."[36] Thus, the principle of conferencing, which took place in the societies and class meetings, was a rational practice and process where transformation and character formation in God's unfolding drama of salvation took place. People's focus on their narcissistic pursuits was refocused on the present but not yet future of God.

As already stated, orthonarrative formation practiced within the church is assisted by participation in the sacrament of Holy Communion. Wesley's view of the sacrament was that it was a means of grace. Within the narrative frame, this means that people encountered God's plot of ongoing salvation, and Holy Communion reinforced the work of connecting the communicants' lives with God's ongoing activity.

Finally, orthonarrative is teleological or purposive and directional.[37] As human beings participate in God's life within the community, they are engaged in God's future. In the world of status anxiety and seeking to affirm one's value and self-validity by giving the self over to worldly values, the end result is destruction and unhappiness. Fortunately, there is an alternative. Orthonarrative or anchoring the self in God's unfolding story of God's present but not yet future is what gives meaning, hope, and purpose to our lives.

35. Runyon, "Orthopathy," 299.
36. Ibid., 300.
37. Ibid., 302.

The purpose of this chapter was to put the practice of orthodoxy or right believing, orthopraxis or right practice, and orthopathy or right feeling into a narrative frame. It is the narrative frame that provides the big picture of God's present but not yet future of establishing God's rule and reign. Wesleyan Christianity for the twenty-first century remains consistent with what God is doing and has been doing throughout human history. God's future is in redeeming creation and persons and in preparing us for God's present but not yet future. There is no need to invest the self ultimately in this perishing world. We must invest in God's world that is present and coming.

Indeed, investing in this world's riches in order to find happiness is a sure-fire pathway to shame. We commit ourselves to this world's definition of human worth and identity, and the end result is that we equate being loved with being wealthy, powerful, class-oriented, prestigious, and popular. Yet, we miss the true source and identity, which comes from God's relationship with us. In relationship to God through Jesus Christ, we find our true worth and identity, and as a result, we transcend shame.

CHAPTER 4

Wesley's Discipline for Guidance in Life

It is clear that there was correspondence between what went on in the society meetings and in the "Minutes of Several Conversations" and the sermons that Wesley delivered. For example, discipline "as common rule of life" developed out of the experiences of John and Charles Wesley along with those of their companions. The discipline that was defined as a common rule of life grew out of their Oxford experiences and their concern for Christian living and formation.[1] Their concern was with Christian practices that could relate to the work and home life of the people in "ordinary towns and villages."[2] What they did in small society meetings and in conferences was all about assisting people to practice discipline. The practice of discipline enabled people to form a relationship with God through Jesus Christ and allowed them to grow through the power of the Holy Spirit into Christian maturity and love of God and of neighbor. Wesley preached sermons, and he published many of these sermons with the expectation that they would be read in society meetings and conferences. What came out of the society meetings often found its way into general rules, minutes, and conversations. These meetings dealt with the practical theological issues with which people were struggling. Thus, Wesley would use these occasions to write minutes, which contained excellent practices of discipline. Moreover, from these meetings, sermons dealing with real life struggles emerged.[3]

---

1. Frank, "Discipline," 245–61.
2. Ibid., 246.
3. Wesley, *Works*, 269–338.

It is clear that Wesley and others saw the connection between what they preached and its relationship to what went on within societies and conferences. For example, in "Minutes of Several Conversations Between the Rev. Mr. Wesley and Others: From the Year 1744 to the Year 1789," the characteristic rhetorical practice of asking questions and providing the answers revealed the close connection Wesley saw between preaching and the internal life within the societies. The question was asked: "Is it advisable for us to preach in as many places as we can, without forming any societies?" The answer provided in these "Minutes" was, "By no means. We have made the trial in various places; and that for a considerable time. But all the seed has fallen as by the highway side. There is scarce any fruit remaining."[4]

Wesley often instructed his ministers to use sermons when teaching within societies. For example, the question was raised: "Why is it that the people under our care are no better?" Wesley answered that it was "because we are not more knowing and more holy."[5] He then went on to recommend that preachers enforce the "Rules of the Society," the "Instructions for Children," and a particular volume of sermons.[6]

The major purpose of this chapter is to make the case that the experiences Wesley and his colleagues underwent as young adults at Oxford are basic needs that all Christians have. The problems of shame and feeling unloved, characteristic of our time, call for the eighteenth-century solutions related to discipline, drawing on nurturing and formational pastoral practices. More specifically, people need to be part of caring communities where they can grow and develop their faith. This is seen clearly in the case of Glenn Henderson, whom we have introduced in earlier chapters.

THE CASE OF GLENN HENDERSON

Glenn Henderson's case demonstrates that one of the major developments following encountering God is the need for fellowship with those more mature in the faith. The goal is to assure progress in the Christian growth and maturity in the process of the faith. It is clear that inherent in

---

4. Ibid., 300.
5. Ibid., 314.
6. Ibid., 315.

the gospel for Wesley and for Glenn Henderson and his wife is the need for growth in the faith. Standing still is not part of Christian formation.

After the collapse of their business, Glenn and his wife Regina returned home to Chicago broken and humiliated. He reached out to family members and began to reconnect with them. Moreover, they began to reach out to others who were more mature in the faith, knowing that God expected them to grow and mature.

Glenn reached out to a man named Richard whom he had known previously. He explained to him that he and his wife were "living nearby and had recently been saved."[7] He learned that Richard and his family "were basically serving as pastors," and occasionally, Glenn and Regina attended church with them.[8] He pointed out that Richard was a "contagious Christian," and Glenn and Regina "were very eager for any meaningful new fellowship."[9] Glenn reported:

> Together, with their immediate extended family and close friends, we decided to meet at his home weekly for fellowship and Bible study. Every week, Regina and I looked forward to going to their home where we would have food, fellowship, and song. For me, this was exactly what I needed and it reminded me of the "early church" and how it was established.

Glenn continued:

> We all felt at ease; the presence of the Holy Spirit was always there and thus we were all transparent. There was no pretense and no judgments—just Christ, grace, forgiveness, love, and acceptance. And yes, there was instruction and lots of prayer.[10]

With this family and their friends, they continued to grow. They realized they were at risk because they were very vulnerable and subject to what they called being tested. Glenn said, "What I did know at that time was that our faith is most tested when there is lack, need, and little."[11] The danger he felt was that, during the vulnerable period, he could have easily been unfaithful or moved backward in his growth. But this group to which he felt accountable helped him to remain faithful

---

7. Henderson, *Treasures*, 199–200.
8. Ibid.
9. Ibid., 200.
10. Ibid., 200–201.
11. Ibid.

and responsive to what God was doing in him and his wife and where God was leading them both.

CONNECTING GLENN AND WESLEY

The need for fellowship so that new converts would grow and not slip back into their previous states was very much on the mind of John Wesley. This is evident in sermon 89, "The More Excellent Way." Wesley was concerned about moving backwards after salvation. He said:

> From long experience and observation I am inclined to think, that whoever finds redemption in the blood of Jesus, whoever is justified, has then the choice of walking in the higher or the lower path. I believe the Holy Spirit at that time sets before him the "more excellent way," and incites him to walk therein; to choose the narrowest path in the narrow way; to aspire after the heights and depths of holiness,—after the entire image of God. But if he does not accept this offer, he insensibly declines into the lower order of Christians.[12]

In the book *Marks of Methodism*, Russell E. Richey, Dennis Campbell, and William Lawrence focus on what they call the third mark of Methodism, which is discipline.[13] This third mark focuses on the disciplined life and holy living related to our behavior within the church, within our private lives, and in our public lives. The concern for discipline as holy living, particularly following justification by grace through faith, often became a problem that had to be addressed for Christians after conversion.

In the quote above, John Wesley makes the statement that those who are justified have the choice of walking in a higher or lower path. The reference Wesley made was to 1 Corinthians 1:31, where those in the church at Corinth were struggling with falling back into cultural forms of self-elevation by identifying the spiritual gifts with categories of status and prestige. This reassertion of self-pride following justification caused many in the Corinthian church to fall into what Wesley called paganism. This was a non-Christian status where persons sought their self-worth by laying their hopes for happiness in the material and secular world. Thus, those who were justified could not move on to

---

12. Wesley, "Way," 6.
13. Richey et al., *Marks*, 67–90.

sanctification because they were still preoccupied with status concerns. Therefore, Wesley's concern was for those in his reading and listening audience to choose the way of love and not to focus on seeking further self-justification and self-validation. Sliding back into their previous states of worldliness prevented them from moving toward the path of greater holiness and happiness in perfecting love, which was the next stage in their spiritual growth.

Moving back into the previous state of seeking self-justification and self-validation through secular and material worldly means was not only a problem during Wesley's time. It is also a problem today. The problem, however, is more insidious in the twenty-first century due to the prevalence of shame. Shame is characterized by the feeling, on a broad scale, of not being valued, worthy, or loved.

The problem in the twenty-first century, however, is that the village is no longer intact, and people cannot make the kinds of choices they need because they feel disconnected, unloved, and worthless. Loss of village connections leads to a sense of being unloved. When people feel unloved and unlovable, their ability to make choices is limited. The only real choice for them is confined to the pursuit of love. Normally, when they feel part of a community, they feel a sense of being valued, and the feeling of value is higher than when disconnected. When avenues for being loved are scarce, however, people seek love in all the wrong places. They often find their pursuit for love frustrating.[14] Even after the gospel is preached and people find that they are embraced by God, they will fall back into the previous patterns of the world unless they become connected to a community where they can be spiritually mentored.

WESLEY'S SMALL GROUP DISCIPLINE

In "The Nature, Design, and General Rules of the United Societies," Wesley pointed out that "eight or ten persons came to me in London; they were deeply convinced of sin and earnestly growing redemption." They asked Wesley to spend "time with them in prayer," and to "advise them how to flee from the wrath to come." Wesley set time aside to work

---

14. *Object relations theory* in the psychoanalytic tradition focuses on the core striving of persons for positive relationships with others. Frustrating relationships with significant others, or the absence of relationships with significant others, can and often will complicate people's ability to make the right choices in their relationships with others. See Hunter, ed., *Dictionary*, 796–98.

with them every week on Thursday evenings. He pointed out that he gave them advice and "concluded our meeting with prayer suited to their several necessities."[15]

The key here is that it is possible to envisage the same need for fellowship that was demonstrated by Glenn and his wife Regina. This basic need for fellowship following conversion is a basic human need in Christianity regardless of the century. Key, however, in contemporary life, is what Thomas E. Frank calls amnesia on the part of many today. That is, such a basic need for fellowship following conversion is often ignored in present-day society. In contrast, Wesley believed that formative Christian practices within small groups were basic to the formation of Christians in the towns and in the villages[16] Ironically, the General Rules that guided the formation in Wesley's day are still contained in the *The Book of Discipline of the United Methodist Church 2008*.[17]

Of significance is the reality that Wesley believed the General Rules were about personal holiness but had to become social holiness "sought in company with others, together with whom one could continue to grow and deepen in good and faithful judgment of how to live as Christian in a complex world."[18] Thus, the General Rules were "structured by practice of studying and conversing in community" in the presence of others where God's grace and Holy Spirit were present.[19]

The logic of the General Rules was the "invitational, relational and developmental" dimension of the Christian life essential to Methodism, according to Frank.[20] Several dimensions related to discipline noted in the General Rules were not only true in Wesley's time, but are true now as well. One element is that people form a covenant "to grow together in the Christian life."[21] The second is calling preachers into conference. The third is the class meeting where conversation or discourse is the central means of grace facilitating a closer relationship with God.

The significance of conversation and discourse as an essential component of Christian practices was the critical element of Wesley's

15. Wesley, *Works*, 269–71.
16. Frank, "Discipline," 246.
17. See *Book of Discipline*, 72–74.
18. Ibid.
19. Franks, "Discipline," 247–48.
20. Ibid., 248.
21. Ibid.

practical theology, which must be carried forward into the twenty-first century. I agree with Frank's assessment that the conversation format is an essential characteristic of Methodism, and it is conversation, together with contemporary narrative theory and rhetoric, which serves to help update Methodist discipline for our contemporary life. Frank concludes:

> As in the logic of the General Rules, a conversation is foremost a relationship and interaction among persons seeking God together, and thus an apprehension of divine grace. If a person is to grow in the knowledge and love of God, s/he must grow in judgment of what is conducive to relationship with God. If a connexion is to grow in effectiveness ministry, it must grow in judgment of what will exhibit the gospel. This growth, whether personal or connexional, occurs through conversation. So Methodist discipline has taught.[22]

In short, conversation is a constituent and formative element central to what it means to be Methodist. It is our distinctive identity, and it is the practice of conversation that was the heart of Wesley's therapeutic and healing practices leading to justification and sanctification.

There is no doubt that the Wesleyan heritage of the practice of conversation must be a central element in responding to the presence of psychological shame, defined as anxiety about whether one is loved or not. The dominant fear of being unloved and thus worthless confirms human beings' lack of identity, and the only way human beings are affirmed is in relationship with others and with God. It is group conversation that provides this element.

Yet, this group conversation is eschatological or hopeful in the twenty-first century because it is connected with the ability of pastoral theological practices to draw persons into God's rule and reign. It is God's ongoing unfolding of God's salvational history for human beings and the world into which we are all drawn. It is in being connected to God's eschatological plot and reign that makes our conversation significant. It is this narrative and plot orientation to practical theology that not only transforms human worth and identity, but also is transforming creation.

It is not just conversation in small groups that made Wesley's practical theology significant. It was also the use of his sermons in the small group that enriched the conversation. Thus, the next section of this chapter explores how Wesley's rhetorical methods of sermon

22. Ibid., 250.

construction kept the nurturing conversation in small groups as their major function.

"THE MORE EXCELLENT WAY"

I will now turn attention away from Wesley's General Rules and draw attention to his therapeutic rhetoric that appeared in the sermon "The More Excellent Way." It is important to remember that in Wesley's practical theology his sermons were often published so that they could be read by those who participated in the small group societies. The use of sermons as well as other practices—such as publishing hymns and liturgies to be used in society meetings along with Wesley's sermons and treatises—was called practical divinity.[23]

He used therapeutic rhetoric to urge those in the audience to take the next developmental step in the salvation process, which was sanctification. Developmentally, those in Wesley's audience had already experienced God's justifying grace. Their sins had been forgiven, and their diseased souls had been healed. In justification, the juridical and therapeutic notions are linked. Guilt from the juridical view is forgiven, and the diseased sin-sick soul from the therapeutic vantage point has been healed. The next step in the developmental and therapeutic movement toward happiness is to continue to grow in God's grace and allow it to carry one to the next level. The next level is sanctification, or perfecting God's love through the concern for living a holy life and showing love to one's neighbors.

The real danger, which Wesley addressed in this sermon, was the concern of backsliding, or movement backwards in the therapeutic process of growth in salvation. Wesley used the word *heathen*, which meant non-Christian in the sense of not actively being Christ-centered. Wesley was well aware that the gains in the salvational process could easily be lost if there were no continued practicing of spiritual discipline.

Wesley began the sermon by reflecting on 1 Corinthians 12:31. He translated the words to read, "Covet earnestly the best gifts: and yet I show unto you a more excellent way."[24] His initial comment on this passage was to refer to Paul's interpretation of the text to Paul's original audience. Here, Wesley was using rhetorical criticism learned in the

---

23. Maddox, "Theology of John and Charles Wesley, 26.
24. Wesley, *Sermons*, vol. 3.

university and within the Anglican Church, and he told his audience that Paul wanted his audience to covet or desire earnestly the gifts of the Spirit. Yet, even in desiring spiritual gifts and exercising them, there was a more excellent way. Wesley said that this more excellent way was infallible and would lead to true happiness. Yet, according to Wesley, in earnestly coveting these divine gifts, it was still possible to be miserable in current time as well as in eternal time. Happiness, contrasted with being miserable, had to do, in Wesley's mind, with not only having access to spiritual gifts, but exercising these gifts on the behalf of Christians and non-Christians. In Wesley's rhetorical attention-getting rhetoric, he alerted his audience to the problem that would occupy the focus of this sermon. That problem was the failure of those in his audience to use the gifts of the Holy Spirit on behalf of those inside and outside the church and Wesleyan societies. This, indeed, was a problem of discipline in the sense of continued practice of the gifts of the Holy Spirit to foster scriptural holiness within the community. The discipline of practicing scriptural holiness referred to those spiritual activities that enabled the practitioner and those being mentored to grow into the image of Christ.

The next rhetorical point in the introduction of the sermon was to connect the disuse of the gifts of the Holy Spirit to the main social problem preventing those in the audience from exercising these gifts. The problem, in Wesley's mind, was the extent to which the church had become socially respectable in the time of Constantine. During the fourth century, the emperor of Rome, Constantine, welcomed all Christians who had been apostates from the faith to return through forgiveness from him. *Apostate*, in this case, refers to the state of denouncing one's faith for the sake of self-interest to prevent being martyred. Despotic emperors prior to Constantine made Christians denounce their allegiance to the Christian church and declare loyalty to the emperor. The end result of the Constantine's forgiveness was a note of social respectability that, in Wesley's mind, made the gifts of the Holy Spirit ineffective. Consequently, his concern was to assure that this did not happen to those in his hearing and reading audience.

What Wesley was addressing in his sermon were the latent results of royal forgiveness that had led to an opportunistic embracing of the honor and shame system of the social evaluation of human worth. To be honorable, people had to identify with what was considered honorable, and this meant wealth, power, prestige, heightened social status, and position. Here again the danger that Wesley addressed in many of his sermons surfaced. This danger was laying up treasures on earth rather than in heaven. Failure to attend to spiritual and heavenly things will cause the gifts of the Holy Spirit to become ineffectual.

The rhetorical problem that Wesley addressed, then, was failure to exercise the gifts of the Holy Spirit because of social respectability. Moreover, Wesley began to move to the next stage of the sermon, which was an exploration of the nature of the problem and how it could be resolved. Here, Wesley addressed the difference between extraordinary gifts and ordinary gifts. Prestige and status would attract people to the extraordinary gifts, and these gifts included the gifts of speaking, persuasion, and so forth. The ordinary gift that all had access was the way of love. This was the more excellent way.

"ON ZEAL"

To this point, three models of Wesley's approach to sin have been explored. The first model was the juridical view of sin, where the motivating factor for change was the fear of condemnation. The second view of sin was a therapeutic view of sin, and the motivating factor leading to God was cure of the sin-sick soul. Here the emphasis was on finding happiness in God as the prime motivation for life. These two models focused on the theme of justification by grace through faith, and people were made right with God due either to fear or to the desire for happiness. The third model was a continuation of the theme of happiness in God, but the difference was in the fear of falling back into a pre-justifying state if one did not grow. The shift in emphasis was on the need to continue to grow, and the motivation was to continue to grow in grace for fear of regressing to the former state. In short, the third model moved from justification to the stage of sanctification, and growth in grace toward perfection. Wesley's fourth model was a continuation of the theme of growing toward perfection, with the motivation shifting, in the sermon "On Zeal," to carefully attend to those deceptions that threaten to prevent further growth in the sanctification process.[25] This fourth model emphasized a narrative understanding of sanctification rather than a therapeutic understanding of sanctification. A narrative view of sanctification focused on growing toward perfection, but not for

25. Wesley, *Wesley's Sermons*, 465–73.

fear of falling back or losing ground. Rather, the focus was on the desire to grow more toward Christlikeness. The emphasis shifted away from fear of loss to the rewards of being Christlike and responding in faith in service to others. In other words, growing in perfecting love became the chief end, and happiness came in knowing one was being faithful to God and executing responsible grace. There was a nuanced shift in emphasis toward the positive benefits resulting from a relationship with divinity and not the negative fear of loss.

The sermon "On Zeal" represents nuanced emphasis, from Wesley's therapeutic model to a narrative emphasis. From Mark Ellingsen's understanding of Wesley's thinking, narrative is the process of movement toward renewing creation and the self through the deification process.[26] It was the ever-growing discipline of becoming like God. It was Christlikeness, and Jesus was the second Adam, who redeemed creation through his incarnation. Thus, narrative theology was the movement toward becoming Christlike. The sermon "On Zeal" revealed how this process of deification worked.

The rhetoric in the sermon "On Zeal" began with the following statement: "There are few subjects in the whole compass of religion that are of greater importance than this. For without zeal it is impossible, either to make any considerable progress in religion whether in temporal or spiritual things."[27] Immediately following this statement, Wesley mentioned emphatically that some dynamic capacity was needed to prevent remaining in the same place. Here, Wesley emphasized that faith required movement and growth in service to one's neighbor both temporally and spiritually. Yet, he further pointed out that the zeal must be of the right kind.

He pointed out that it was possible to distinguish between good zeal and bad zeal because of the deceitfulness of the human heart.[28] Human passions have the capacity to be self-justifying, and Wesley felt that very little attention had been given to how to discern between good and bad zeal. Rhetorically, therefore, his task in the sermon was to convince those in his reading and listening audience to differentiate Christian zeal from counterfeit zeal. Obviously Wesley felt urgency to address this important problem because it was central to his notion of

---

26. Ellingsen, *Reclaiming*, 71.
27. Wesley, *Wesley's Sermons*, 465.
28. Ibid., 466.

growth and development in salvation, namely through sanctification, or growing toward perfection.

Following the rhetoric of the motivational sequence, Wesley sought to address the problem of distinguishing good and bad zeal by making three points. He sought to describe the nature of Christian zeal, to delineate its properties, and to help his audience visualize the practical implications of his analysis.

He began by defining the meaning of zeal in the Greek language, found in Galatians 4:18. He pointed out that Christian zeal was the passion or desire on behalf of a religious object or end.[29] What made zeal religious was charity or love, according to Wesley. Love was the chief ingredient in Christian zeal. It was the love of God and the love of neighbor. It followed that the properties of love were the properties of zeal.

The rhetoric of persuading through emphasis on reward rather than on fear pointed to pre-Enlightenment influence on Wesley's thought. First, being in relationship with God, in pre-Enlightenment thought, emphasized the benefits of such a relationship, and the benefits were not only happiness. They also were the development of religious virtues and characteristics.[30] The emphasis was on human flourishing as the result of being in relationship with God, and this flourishing had everything to do with translating this flourishing into one's relationship to one's neighbor. The qualities that benefited neighborliness included humility, meekness, patience, and giving the self over to divine providence, or, in Wesley's thought, trusting God, knowing that everything would work out fine in one's love of neighbor.

Flourishing in personal growth and development was possible because the relationship permeated one's entire soul and holy tempers resulted, according to Wesley's practical theological thought. Holy tempers included long-sufferance, gentleness, meekness, fidelity, temperance, and the mind that was in Christ.[31] God was at the center of the human heart. Works of mercy and works of piety became the activity as a result.

Not only could one see the happiness and flourishing model present in this sermon, it was also possible to envisage the influence of Irenaeus' narrative theological thinking. Ellingsen suggests that it is

29. Ibid., 466–67.
30. Charry, *By the Renewing of Your Minds*, 3.
31. Wesley, *Wesley's Sermons*, 467–68.

possible to see clearly Irenaeus' narrative theological influence of eastern Christianity on Wesley's thinking.[32] Narrative meant movement and process. Flourishing, resulting from being in relationship with God, led also to the development of holy tempers and works of mercy and works of piety. Works of mercy included attending to the souls and bodies of others, or to their spiritual and physical needs. Works of piety included "reading and hearing the word, public, family, and private prayers, receiving the Lord's Supper, fasting or abstinence."[33]

The significance of Wesley's connection with Irenaeus and Wesley's understanding of zeal is the relation of narrative rhetoric to the central dynamic of sanctification. Narrative rhetoric not only depicts movement and process; it also highlights the central dynamic of the pull and the drawing power of narrative. The power of Scripture is in its ability to get the hearer or reader to suspend his or her own way of seeing reality and, as the reader or hearer is drawn in, to take on the world as it is revealed in the text.[34] The key is that Scripture draws the reader or hearer into the plot that lies behind the stories and narratives, and this plot is the unfolding of God's rule and reign through the transformation and recreation of the world through Jesus Christ and the call of the church universal. This is not to say that Wesley understood Scripture in this way. It is to say, however, that Wesley understood the dynamic nature of Scripture, and his concept of Scriptural holiness pointed to the dynamic and powerful nature of Scripture. The point is that Wesley did not employ the plot logic of Scripture as the central dynamic of his understanding of the doctrine of sanctification.

Mark Elllingsen, however, points out that in a number of Wesley's sermons he demonstrated that he understood the powerful impact Scripture had on the lives of those who hear biblical stories retold in sermons. Ellingsen points out that in a number of sermons Wesley "identifies his hearers with characters in the biblical accounts."[35] Ellingsen identifies Wesley's sermon "Upon Our Lord's Sermon on the Mount," from 1739, where Wesley likened his readers and hearers to the lives of

---

32. Ellingsen, *Reclaiming*, 72–73.

33. Wesley, *Wesley's Sermons*, 468.

34. The following books help to show the development of a biblical narrative approach, which is the basis of narrative rhetorical criticism: Ellingsen, *Integrity*, 18–52; Goldberg, *Theology and Narrative*; Wimberly, *Using Scripture*.

35. Ellingsen, *Integrity*, 48.

Pharisees.[36] Indeed, Wesley made the identification for the reader, but the key emphasis made here, however, is on the reader or hearer being drawn into the text through the power of the text itself. The focus of contemporary narrative rhetoric is the power of Scripture, as story, to draw human beings into the dynamic, unfolding plot of God.

WESLEY AND THE TWENTY-FIRST CENTURY

The aim of this chapter has been to explore the significance for the twenty-first century of Wesley's thought about the juridical and therapeutic understanding of salvation. More specifically, the concern was to explore the implications of this model for dealing with the modern experience of shame as the feeling of being disconnected resulting in the feeling of being unloved. Our examination of Wesley's rational rhetorical approach revealed that his thought contained elements of narrative rhetorical criticism. This is especially true regarding process and movement as Wesley tried to draw people into the biblical narrative itself. It was the conclusion, however, that Wesley's narrative orientation was not narrative rhetoric in the sense of emphasizing the power of Scripture to draw hearers and readers into the text and to convince them to adopt plot logic and the world as disclosed by Scripture.[37] While Wesley assumed that the biblical world was different from the secular world, the rhetorical power of the biblical world was assumed, but not part of his actual method of doing practical theology.

Yet, the power of Wesley's thought holds out great promise to speak to contemporary life and, especially, to the problem of shame. Narrative rhetorical methods of persuasion will do three things for Wesley's thought. First, they will bring out the significance of Wesley's understanding of discipline as Scriptural holiness. Second, they will show how narrative rhetoric enhances communal participation and adds to the important notions of recreating Methodist societies and congregations.

36. Ibid.

37. This view of Wesley coincides with what Mark Ellingsen wrote in correspondence with me about Wesley. In this sense, Wesley was not pre-modern. Ellingsen writes, "When I refer to a pre-modern narrative approach, I am thinking in terms of my Yale mentors (Hans Frei, Brevard Childs, and George Lindbeck) who were very Barthian. For them, this approach entails that you begin with the Word of God and lure the hearer/reader into the story. When that happens, the believer's prior experience and questions are overcome/transformed by God's word and the narrative." This correspondence was in an email dated August 31, 2009.

Finally, they will show how narrative rhetoric speaks to the contemporary problem of human shame.

First, narrative rhetoric will show how being in relationship to God through Jesus Christ and the resultant happiness and the virtues of love of neighbor are not only reinforced by Scripture, but are also nurtured by Scripture. Attending to Scripture as story, and emphasizing its power to draw and to pull persons into God's unfolding plot, supports and enhances what God does to the believer in relational discourse. Scriptural holiness becomes development of works of mercy and works of piety resulting from being drawn into God's unfolding salvational plot.

By talking about the power of Scripture to draw human beings into the story and to get them to suspend their customary ways of seeing reality, the emphasis is on a pre-modern understanding of the power of Scripture. According to Ellingsen, the absence of this sense of the power of Scripture in Wesley made Wesley modern rather than pre-modern. Therefore, the suggestion of this author is that Wesley's use for today is in recovering more fully the pre-modern sense of Scripture.[38]

Second, narrative rhetoric by its very nature is communal. Narrative rhetoric assumes that Scripture itself is a living community of persons, with God encountering a living community of persons. Scripture is communion with the saints and God. The power of narrative is that it requires storytellers and story-listeners. This was the significance of the Wesleyan societies wherein people could find a safe space for their stories to unfold and wherein all involved could see God's work at the center of their lives. Wesley's original vision of a small, nurturing society needs to be enhanced by an understanding of the drawing power of Scripture as well as by the small community of mutual interpreters of what God is doing to sustain the sanctification process.

Narrative rhetoric also helps those within the societies to envisage the interconnection between justification and sanctification. There are other interconnections, including the personal and communal, practices of personal piety and practices of mercy to others, and the interconnections of the individual and communal lives of persons in these societies.

Finally, narrative rhetoric through biblical storytelling and story-listening in the daily lives of those societies, helps to respond to the shame that characterizes modern experience. Pastoral counseling and psychology reveal that people who are disconnected are looking for a

---

38. Ellingsen, *Integrity*, 48.

safe place to tell their stories. The narrative rhetorical model embraces the psychological model of shame, which relates to the person's need for love rather than to his or her guilt. Rhetorical narrative does not neglect guilt. Rather, it recognizes that addressing guilt first often blocks the natural emergence of guilt once people feel loved and cared for. Pastoral counseling and pastoral psychology reveal that people are freed up to discuss their self-sabotaging behavior when they genuinely feel embraced and loved by others.

Indeed, updating of Wesley's rhetoric of reason with narrative rhetoric holds out a great deal of promise for making his thinking relevant for the twenty-first century. It is the next task of this work to address Wesley's public theology, or his attempt to address public issues through his treatises.

CHAPTER 5

Shame, Slavery, and Economics of Hope
Wesley's Public Theology

> I see not how you can go through your glorious enterprise in opposing that execrable villainy which is the scandal of religion, of England, and of human nature. Unless God has raised you up for this very thing, you will be worn out by the opposition of men and devils. But if God be for you, who can be against you? Are all of them together stronger than God? O be not weary of well doing! Go on, in the name of God and in the power of his might, till even American Slavery (the vilest that ever saw the sun) shall vanish away before it.
>
> Reading this morning a tract wrote by a poor African, I was particularly struck by the circumstance that a man who has a black skin, being wronged or outraged by a white man, can have no redress; it being a "law" in our colonies that the oath of a black against a white goes for nothing?[1]

THIS QUOTE FROM JOHN Wesley was taken from a letter to William Wilberforce, who was a member of the British Parliament. In the letter, Wesley encouraged him to take action for change against the vile system of slavery.[2] England outlawed participation in slave trading in 1807.

In this chapter, I aim to show that Wesley saw a connection between human bondage and its impact on the souls of those who did the enslaving as well as on those who were enslaved. He saw that earning

---

1. Wesley, *Journal and Diaries*, 7:242.

2. Hempton, "Wesley in Context," 72; Campbell, "Wesley as Diarist and Correspondent," 130; and Miles, "Happiness, Holiness, and the Moral," 217.

one's living and wellbeing at the expense of others was the major source of sin. Thus, the primary basis of his rhetorical practices dealing with slavery was his awareness that one's wellbeing in life ultimately did not depend on one's economic wellbeing, but was based on the One who created the economy in the first place.

The significance of this chapter for our contemporary society is that we can learn—from past traditions of faith and what they have to teach us—about the limitations of investing our happiness totally in "this world's" economic systems. Moreover, they teach us that our happiness as human beings cannot rest on the backs of other human beings. More precisely, it is not possible to gain identity by forcing others into human shame and humiliation in order to bolster human privilege and economic superiority at the expense of others. Rather, our happiness rests in responding to God's love for us through love and service to others. Therefore, after this chapter introduces Wesley's rhetorical devices to address the evils of slavery, I will introduce the implications of Wesley's thoughts on slavery for the twenty-first century. The first implication will address how injustice challenges those being oppressed to confine their worth and identity as human beings to earthly, cultural, derogatory, shaming, and damaging images of their humanity and worth. Secondly, the chapter will address the implications of Wesley's practical theology for addressing unjust economic systems of exploitation.

It is key that we not only can visualize Wesley's therapeutic and healing dimension of this salvation theology at work, but also can see his juridical or justice-oriented theology in which people are held accountable for their sin. Wesley sought to help heal the damages inflicted on black people as a result of slavery as well as to heal the identities of white slave owners who sought their worth and identity at the expense of others. He also wanted slave owners to realize that their efforts to achieve identity, power, authority, and economic security on a faulty economic system was also sinful, for which they would suffer judgment.

WESLEY'S EVANGELICAL RHETORICAL GOAL

Wesley's rhetorical and practical theological goal was not to make Christian public theologians who were politically aware citizens. In fact, becoming public theologians was a latent effect of his effort to save souls. His goal was evangelical, and he wanted all human beings to have a personal relationship with God as well as to respond to God's grace at work in their lives through loving God, self, and neighbor. Indeed, this chapter takes very seriously Robin Lovin's conclusion that Wesley's primary agenda was fostering a relationship with God.[3] In fact, Lovin states:

> Wesley strongly opposed slavery, not because he believed that "all men are created equal," but because he believed that the slave, like everyone else, has a soul that can be addressed, claimed, and redeemed by God. Thus the slave, like everyone else, needs the freedom to respond to the word of grace proclaimed. The equality that Wesley understood was evangelical, not political, and he probably would have understood claims to human dignity on behalf of sinners in need of conversion as a positive hindrance to the reception of the gospel.[4]

Wesley believed slavery hindered and blocked human beings' relationship with God. It made it difficult for those who enslaved others to trust in God who was the source of the enslaver's true identity, worth, and dignity. It also made it difficult for those who were enslaved to feel close to God due to being enslaved by other human beings.

Wesley understood that slavery as a system and slave trading as an ideology were grounded in a *this-world*-oriented narrative that sought human happiness, identity, worth, and dignity at the expense of other human beings. To base one's identity and worth at the expense of others was sin and idolatry for Wesley. Moreover, this sin and idolatry had horrific consequences for others. Thus, slavery and slave trading put the salvation of the slave owner and the slave trader at peril just as it did those who were enslaved. As a result, Wesley felt he had to convince the slave owner and trader that their economic practices put their souls in jeopardy just as it did the souls of those enslaved. Therefore, Wesley's rhetoric of persuasion not only dealt with the soul and sin, but also with the economic system. His fundamental concern was to get the slave owner and trader to adopt a new form of economics that did not lay one's hope for happiness and worth on this world's exploitive and oppressive economic system.

Wesley was all about developing an economics of hope that freed black people in slavery as well as liberated whites who enslaved others. At the foundation of his theology for combating slavery was his therapeutic and healing model of salvation. His healing and therapeutic

---

3. Lovin, "Human Rights, Vocation, and Human Dignity," 109–23.
4. Ibid., 115.

salvation theology speaks volumes to the twenty-first-century understanding of shame as well as the humiliation caused by colonialism and the economic efforts of whites who enslaved blacks to gain worth and identity by exploiting others.

For the economic system of slavery to work, slave owners and traders felt they had to stigmatize black people in slavery by labeling them as less than human and no better than animals. Wesley saw how this system of stigmatization was a major obstacle for the black person in slavery's relationship with God through Jesus Christ. Moreover, slavery was also was a form of idolatry blocking the enslavers' relationship with God as well. In short, slavery functioned as a method of reinforcing the humiliation and shame that destroyed not only the worth of those in slavery, but also the worth and value of those who owned slaves and practiced slave trading. It was only in a relationship with God in Jesus Christ that true worth and value was bestowed. Because slavery destroyed the souls and happiness of two races of people, Wesley was convinced that this economic system had to be abolished.[5]

Wesley and Public Rhetoric

Wesley had a simple motivational rhetoric. It was addressed directly to those in his reading and hearing audiences. George Lawton examines Wesley's literary roles as a publicist. A publicist is one who addresses public events through preaching, letter-writing, and producing educational tracts, as a diarist, pamphleteer, critic, and editor.[6] Lawton concludes that Wesley's homiletic and writing styles used a very simple rhetorical framework. Wesley told the audience what he intended to do, then he executed his intention, and finally, he told the reader and listener that he had completed his task.[7] He says Wesley's rhetoric in sermons had a therapeutic diagnostic precision, possessing clinical insight and accuracy. He used this therapeutic rhetoric to connect with his audience.[8] His use of prose was ordinary, and his language was always crystal clear, appropriate, penetrating, reasoned, and yet persuasive.[9]

---

5. Marquardt, "Social Ethics," 294–96.
6. Lawton, *Wesley's English*, 240–65.
7. Ibid., 240.
8. Ibid., 242.
9. Ibid., 244.

He was careful to adopt the people's common language, assuring that he would bond and communicate with them.[10]

Moreover, his sermons, as well as his vast publications, found their way into the homes of people and were part of many informal and formal conversations. In other words, his rhetoric was not just therapeutic. It was also a nurturing rhetoric, which nurtured the growth of persons as they were led by God's spirit into perfect love. His writings and thoughts were very much part of the public arena, both inside and outside the church. He could have been what social ethicist Robert Franklin calls a public theologian, particularly since he brought his faith unapologetically into the public arena.[11]

Lawton points out that Wesley's thoughts and writings were public news in the eighteenth century. In fact, he says:

> Methodism was news. Largely by what Wesley called "singularity," i.e. full-blooded Christianity which contrasted noticeably with formal churchmanship—Methodism made an impact upon almost every community. As news, it stirred many a pen up and down the country.[12]

Wesley wrote excellent tracts or treatises where he appealed to public religious common sense and reason. He would make his persuasive conclusions, drawing on the religious understanding common at that time.

Wesley's characteristic therapeutic and nurturing rhetorical style was to grab the attention of his audience immediately. This was the case in this treatise. He declared immediately in the first paragraph his transparent intent to give a plain account of his religious principles and actions, trusting his innate writing wisdom that this would be the most appropriate way to connect with his reading audience.[13] In the second paragraph, he indicated the problem he would address in the treatise. He drew the audience's focus to "numerous follies" and miseries of human beings who had no religion or whose religion was lifeless and formal. He, then, pointed out that it would be great if it were possible to convince those people that God gifted humanity with religion. Not only was religion a gift, it was the source that gave human kind the love of God,

10. Ibid., 245.

11. Franklin, "Travelin Shoes," 3, and *Another Day's Journey*. See also Wimberly, *Care and Counseling*, 126–27.

12. Lawton, *Wesley's English*, 260.

13. Wesley, *Works*, 3.

the source of all good and love in life. God loved us first, and God was the fountain of all good we hope to enjoy.[14]

To summarize, Wesley's practices of persuasion were therapeutic in the sense that they sought to heal the sin of those seeking to establish human identity and happiness at the expense of others. This sin was evident in the oppressive slave-based economic system and in slave trading.

WESLEY'S PUBLIC RHETORIC AND PROTEST AGAINST INJUSTICE

About two-thirds of the way through his *Thoughts Upon Slavery*, it is clear that Wesley's rhetorical techniques changed to a diatribe, which marked his shift away from the rhetoric of nurturing and therapy to a combative argumentative strategy to refute slavery.[15] It is clear that Wesley was making an impassioned argument, heightening an emotional rhetoric. He emphasized that there was a clear difference between justice and injustice and between cruelty and mercy. He talked about the injustice of taking Africans from their native land removing the rights guaranteed to all Englishmen.

His major premise was that all slave holding was inconsistent with natural justice. It was inconsistent with mercy. He attacked the profit motive and stressed that it was the heart of slavery. The most significant argumentative challenge, however, was his point that slavery was an idolatrous economic system where those who engaged in it laid up for themselves treasures on earth and sought happiness through riches. He relied heavily on his ultimate premise, which was all happiness and virtue began with God and certainly did not rest in the slave-based economic system.

In this shift to diatribe, Wesley changed to what Carey calls the emotional rhetoric of sentimentality. This radical shift separated Wesley's approach from the rhetoric of Benezet. In part 4 of his treatise on slavery, he began with this shift of rhetoric, and it continued to the very end of the tract. In addition, Wesley continued his rhetorical diatribe by confronting vigorously the slave traders' slaving activities. He indicated that he would address his main writing audience, the captains of the slave ships, the merchants who dealt in slave trading, and the planters

---

14. Ibid.
15. Jewett, *Romans*, 25. Here, Jewett describes diatribe as a combative strategy.

who extracted free labor from those enslaved. He made sure that those in his audiences in England and in the American colonies knew that he was addressing them.

Wesley clearly stated his first and second premise theologically in the form of a question and then an answer. He said:

> Is there a God? You know there is. Is he a just God? Then there must be a state of retribution; a state wherein the just God will reward every man according to his works. Then what reward will he render to you? O think betimes! Before you drop into eternity! Think now, "He shall have judgment without mercy that showed no mercy."[16]

In his last direct comment to them after indicating that liberty was a human natural right, he wrote the following words:

> If, therefore, you have any regard to justice, (to say nothing of mercy, nor the revealed law of God,) render unto all their due. Give liberty to whom liberty is due, that is, to every child of man, to every partaker of human nature. Let none serve you but by his own act and deed, by his own voluntary choice. Away with all whips, all chains, all compulsion! Be gentle toward all men; and see that you invariably do unto every one as you would he should do unto you.[17]

After the above statement, he prayed a prayer of petition, not on behalf of the ship captains, merchants, or planters; rather, he addressed those blacks who had been enslaved.

> O thou God of love, thou who are loving to every man, and whose mercy is over all thy works; thou who are the Father of the spirits of all flesh, and who are rich in mercy unto all; thou who has mingled of one blood all the nations upon earth; have compassion upon these outcasts of men, who are trodden down as dung upon the earth! Arise, and help these that have no helper, whose blood is spilt upon the ground like water! Are not these also the work of thine own hands, the purchase of thy Son's blood? Stir them up to cry unto thee in the land of their captivity; and let their complaint come up before thee; let it enter into thy ears! Make even those that lead them away captive to pity them, and turn their captivity as the rivers in the south. O burst thou all their chains in sunder;

---

16. Wesley, "Thoughts."
17. Ibid.

more especially the chains of their sins! Thou Savior of all, make them free, that they may be free indeed![18]

The most significant dimension of this prayer was Wesley's theological connection between the need for justice and evangelism. Wesley comprehended that slavery and slave trading hindered God's work in the lives of all persons, and slavery blocked and hindered the enslaved black people's relationship with God as well as the slaveholder or slave trader's own relationship with God by engaging in the slave-based economic system. Theologically, Wesley did not separate the souls of human beings from their economic, political, social, and cultural situation. Persons were whole human beings, and their souls and spirits interacted with their social and cultural context. Thus, Wesley expected those who based their entire system of survival on the backs of others to be judged harshly by God, and they needed to renounce their evil ways or face retribution.

From my own rhetorical analysis above, it is clear that my conclusions about Wesley's authorship of *Thoughts Upon Slavery* are very similar to Carey's conclusions. Indeed, Wesley followed the work of Benezet, and the rhetoric employed by Benezet was very logical and rational. This was the case in the first three sections, but the rhetoric shifted dramatically in the fourth and fifth sections of the treatise. I used the rhetorical term diatribe to describe Wesley's shift, but I like Carey's use of the term *sentimental rhetoric* to describe the shift in rhetoric. This dramatic change separated the writing of Wesley in the tract from the writing style of Benezet.

Carey concludes that Wesley's work departed from the geographical and legal (rational) argument, and utilized rhetoric of the heart to match Wesley's emphasis on feeling religion.[19] I agree with Carey that his rhetoric not only shifted toward the literary use of emotion and sentimentality, but it shifted away from a political tract to an enthusiastic political sermon characteristic of Wesley's ecclesiastical context and ethos.

Of critical significance is Carey's statement that Wesley brought his private "feelings into the public sphere."[20] This made Wesley a "sentimental hero" or "a man of feeling." Carey says that this was an "ironic

---

18. Ibid.
19. Carey, "Wesley's *Thoughts*," 283.
20. Ibid.

strategy, and the true implied reader" in Wesley's audience was a feeling person, or one who was "shocked by the slave owner's brute insensibility because he has the sensibility required to be capable of being shocked in that way."[21] In short, Carey is suggesting that Wesley's intended reading audience were those persons who would be moved by Wesley's compassion. I must say that there must have been women who would have been reading this tract in the general public as well as in the society meetings.

Carey also indicates that eighteenth-century rhetorical sentimentality rested on the capacity of the writer and speaker to generate empathy, or the ability to imagine the feelings of another.[22] This relates to what I have identified in earlier places as therapeutic rhetoric, known as the motivational sequence. This was a major characteristic in all of Wesley's sermons. The motivational sequence was the effort to identify the concern or problem with which the audience was struggling and then address it in the sermon. Thus, Wesley's use of the language of the heart is consistent with his rhetorical style in other sermons.

WESLEY AND THE TWENTY-FIRST CENTURY BLACK COMMUNITY

Wesley was concerned that slavery had an impact on the souls of the black people who were enslaved. I was struck considerably by Wesley's ending of "Thoughts Upon Slavery." Suddenly, the tract ended with a prayer, which focused on the captivity of those enslaved without addressing the slave owners who were the subject of the tract. I not only noticed this sudden shift, but I also noticed the ending poem, which, frankly, upset me. He used what I thought were anger triggering and inciting words that would be totally unacceptable to twentieth-century and twenty-first-century African Americans. The poem was written as follows:

> The servile progeny of Ham
> Seize as the purchase of the blood!
> Let all the Heathens know thy name:
> From idols to the living God
> The dark Americans convert,
> And shine in every pagan heart![23]

---

21. Ibid., 284.
22. Ibid.
23. Wesley, "Thoughts."

I was suspicious of his identifying of enslaved Africans with Ham to justify slavery in the American colonies, but I was also disturbed by the word *pagan*. I was ready to dismiss Wesley as a modern-day typical racist who believed in the inferiority of black people. I was so disturbed that I looked up the term pagan, and discovered it was not a derogatory term, but a descriptive word for non-Christians. He was not using it in the sense of the word *heathen*, which in racist language was derogatory, implying or meaning uncivilized. The word heathen was used to justify the ill treatment of black people in slavery. It is clear that Wesley was not using the term pagan to justify slavery. Wesley even used the word heathen earlier in the tract, but it was in the sense of non-Christian and not uncivilized.

Yet, I remained mystified by his relating black folk with the cursed children of Ham, however, until I read J. Gordon Melton's account of Wesley's impact on slavery in the American colonies, and Warren Thomas Smith's assessment of Wesley on slavery, as well as Carey's account of Wesley's rhetoric.[24] As a result, my spirit became more forgiving, and I could embrace Wesley's genuine concern for the black enslaved as well as for their freedom from captivity.

The shift to this poem at the end of the treatise on slavery was unexpected, and it seemed out of place. Rhetorically, however, it made sense. Wesley's rhetoric always took into account those who would be reading his treatises. Therefore, he was addressing not the slave owners or slave traders, exclusively. Rather, he was addressing those in the societies and those in the public who might be persuaded by his anti-slavery and anti-slave-trade sentiments. Therefore, he wanted to be sure that they saw the connection between slavery and its slave trade and the negative impact both had on those enslaved. I am sure his rhetoric was to incite in his audience moral outrage against slavery.

When I look at the implications of Wesley's rhetoric for the twenty-first century, I also think of persons who might be interested in Wesley's thoughts on slavery in congregations. How would we translate Wesley's rhetoric so that we in this century can visualize the significance of Wesley's thoughts for today? First, it is important to envisage modern-day segregation, prejudice, and beliefs in the inferiority of people of

---

24. Warren Thomas Smith indicated that "Thoughts Upon Slavery" was Wesley's genuine work (*Wesley and Slavery*, 91); Melton, *Will to Choose*, 25; Carey, "Wesley's Thoughts," 284.

color as a political process. As a political process these negative activities and convictions seek to restrict the access of people of color to the limited economic resources offered by society. I understand racial politics as "limiting access to the vast range yet finite supply of resources needed for human fulfillment."[25]

Wesley dealt with overt racism and forceful and oppressive enslavement of Africans in the colonies and in England. One subtle and less overt strategy used today among the white majority is to recruit African Americans, Hispanic Americans, Asian Americans, and immigrant Americans of color into negative stereotypes so that they internalize these negative images. When these negative stereotypes are internalized by these groups, the devalued people become less of a threat economically.

To say this in Wesleyan language, negative images of people of color today help people of color to define themselves as inferior and "less than" others. The end result is settling for jobs and roles in society that majority people do not want. In the Wesleyan spirit, this internalization of the negative images of themselves causes devalued people to limit their identity and worth to these negative and stereotypical images. When this happens, the danger is that this internalizing blocks people of color from seeing themselves as children of God. Thus, the same end result takes place, whether it was overt slavery or subtle recruitment into negative images.

From the standpoint of practical theology in the Wesleyan spirit, Wesley's rhetoric is still applicable for those who are the white majority. His evangelical language would include being concerned about one's neighbor. It would also include the awareness that restricting others to limited economic resources is developing one's group identity and worth at the expense of other, less valued groups. This is indeed sin, but it also damages the soul of those who employ these negative images as well as being detrimental to those who are victims of such negative images.

WESLEY AND TWENTY-FIRST CENTURY CAPITALISM

Another twentieth-century and twenty-first-century concern is whether Wesley's thoughts really addressed the structural issues related to the capitalistic economic system that was emerging as a result of the

---

25. Wimberly, *Care and Counseling*, 12.

burgeoning Industrial Revolution. One assessment of how Wesley addressed the structural issue was given by Manfred Marquardt. His goal was to assess John Wesley's thinking about individual and collective economic ethics. Marquardt believes that all of Wesley's economic thinking rested on Wesley's three simple rules of "gain all you can; save all you can; and give all you can." He stated: "In fact, these rules appropriately sum up Wesley's own practices and his congregational teachings concerning handling money and other economic goods."[26]

The third rule, which focused on giving all you could, was key in Wesley's thinking. Indeed, this rule was focused on making sure that human beings did not lay up their treasures on earth and that they kept their eyes focused on God's present but not yet rule and reign.[27] Placing one's hope for identity, meaning, and happiness in this world's treasures was clearly a tragic choice, and it would eventuate in disastrous consequences in a person or community's life.

Marquardt sought to explore to what extent Wesley's thinking eventually led people to embrace the capitalistic spirit. His concern was to assess whether or not those who followed Wesley embraced the first two of the economic rules, which were to earn all you could, and save all you could. Marquardt clearly believed, as Wesley did, that the third rule—giving all you could—would prevent people laying up for themselves treasures on earth.

Marquardt, however, came to the conclusion that Wesley did contribute to the spread of capitalism. However, while there were some aspects of Wesley's thinking that contributed to the spirit of capitalism, Marquardt believes that Wesley's theology countered this effort to embrace capitalism. He concluded:

> At the same time it must be observed that some fundamental expressions of Wesley's economic ethics thoroughly contradicted the "spirit of capitalism" and, historically considered, worked against that spirit. Alongside the radial social obligation connected with property ownership, these elements specifically included demands that the state intervene in the economic process (to be considered in the next section), and rejection of coupling economic success to favorable standing with God. Indeed, Wesley

---

26. Marquardt, *Wesley's Ethics*, 35.
27. Wesley, "Danger," 1–15.

gave no sign of proving the certainty of faith by good works or earthly prosperity, in the sense of practical syllogism.[28]

I agree with Marquardt's assessment of Wesley's thoughts on economics. Yet, in Marquardt's assessment of Wesley's thoughts on capitalism, he demonstrates that Wesley's ethical thinking clearly addressed some of the structural dimensions of capitalism. It was clearly important to participate in the economic system so that the basic needs of human beings could be met. Yet, placing one's hope for happiness and identity in the economic system was shortsighted and self-deceptive.

Overall, however Marquardt did not believe Wesley really addressed social structural issues. There is some thinking that Wesley did not try to change social structure, and that he was only interested in the souls of the poor. This was Marquardt's conclusion. He says that Wesley rejected structural changes in society.[29] However, Wesley's concern for the souls of the oppressed, his tract "Thoughts Upon Slavery," and his passionate rhetorical diatribe against slavery had the impact of leading the Methodist movement to attack the evils of slavery. This impetus helped to bring slave trading to an end in England.

I am convinced that Wesley's addressing structural dimensions of ethical living is clear in Wesley's practical theology dealing with the injustice of slavery and slave trading. Slavery was a vital reality for Wesley and for his time period, both in England and in the American colonies. It is important to address how Wesley's evangelical theology, grounded in justification and sanctification, had an impact on social structural issues related to slavery. For African Americans living in the twenty-first century, this is the most important issue for testing whether Wesley's theology and thinking are relevant for our contemporary faith and practice.

Scholars' assessments concerning the transforming aspect of his thoughts on slavery are mixed. Some say his thoughts have had a transforming impact on social structures. Others say there was no real impact at all.[30] I take the stand that Wesley's pre-Enlightenment rhetoric was an engaged and a relationally reasoned rhetoric, which did not artificially

---

28. Marquardt, *Wesley's Ethics*, 41–42.

29. Ibid, 134.

30. Meeks, "Home," 1–10; Lovin, "Rights, Vocation, and Dignity," 109–23; Jennings, *Good News*, 181–98; Marquardt, *Wesley's Ethics*, 133–38; and Heitzenrater, "Poor and People," 15–38.

separate reason and experience. Wesley always kept reason and revelation connected and did not join reason only with sense data as did John Locke, whose thinking Wesley understood and challenged. Pre-modern thinking trusted the relationship between the knower and the One who provided the knowledge, and this thinking also envisioned the link between knowledge and virtue. In fact, Wesley's view of revelation and reason as coming from God and leading to virtue in life was his basic point in "Earnest Appeal to Men of Reason and Religion." The point is that Wesley's thoughts did not artificially separate evangelically relating to God through Jesus Christ and a person's responsibility to demonstrate that relationship by living responsibly. Moreover, this spread of Wesley's emphasis on the relationship between the personal processes of justification and sanctification in the societies meant that people within those societies would implement his ideas in their daily lives, depending on their stations in life. The effort of the societies was to help people to internalize the virtues that came from their relationship with God and to live them out in the world.

Further support for connecting evangelical emphasis and social transformation come from some African American political scientists. Contemporary, African American, political science thinking addresses the connection of social transformation and personal transformation. For example, there is a connection, tie, bond, and correlation between personal agency and facilitating the agency of others in the evangelical thinking of African American Christians. Frederick C. Harris points out this causal relationship between the two. The discovery of personal efficacy or agency occurs when an individual realizes that he or she has power to influence his or her condition in life. Then he or she becomes civically involved on behalf of others, illustrating the facilitation of agency. This was particularly the case with African Americans.[31]

Realizing, from my experience as an African American Christian, that there is a holistic connection between personal transformation and engagement in social and political transformation, I was led to look for these same connections in Wesley. Wesley's emphasis on neighborly love, which was a response to God's justifying love, was enacted communally. In the societies, his sermons and tracts were systematically studied. Readers were expected not only to internalize the values and virtues in their lives, but also to live them out in their daily lives and their work.

31. Harris, *Something Within*, 81–85. See also Wimberly, *Care and Counseling*, 28–36.

Therefore, Wesley's thinking was not just for the personal edification of believers. They were expected to make a social witness against slavery. In fact, this was the conclusion of some Wesley historians, as we shall see later in this essay.

SUMMARY AND CONCLUSIONS

This chapter began with the statement that Wesley's primary goal was not to make public theologians. On the contrary his practical theological goal was to enable all persons to have a meaningful relationship with God. Wesley was concerned, however, with the reality that slavery hindered those enslaved from having a meaningful relationship with God. I indicated that Wesley's publicly addressing slavery from his evangelical perspective would have latent consequences and eventually would change the slave system. My analysis not only confirms this, but also confirms, validates, and reinforces Wesley's conscious effort to possibly change social structure by moving what Cary called the implied reader to consider addressing the slave trade as an economic system.

My contention in this chapter is that Wesley's pre-Enlightenment theology, focusing on happiness and virtue, permitted him to do public theology in a way that held evangelism and political action together. The use of relational, nurturing, emotional, rhetorical, and diatribe theory, applied to Wesley's sermons and tracts, helps to illustrate his holistic approach. His concern for the relationship of persons to God, as well as his speaking to the need for virtuous love in addressing public issues of vital concern for all, were consistent. For me, his commitment to the abolitionist movement to end slavery needs to be the center of all of our efforts to understand Wesley as a public theologian.

A final point needs to be mentioned about Wesley and those enslaved in the American colonies. According to Love Henry Whelchel, Wesley's ministry in the Americas from 1735 to 1737 was significant for Wesley and subsequently influenced his work to abolish the slave system. He endeared himself to those Africans in slavery in the Americas because of his concern for their welfare, physical and spiritual. In fact, Whelchel points out that the popularity of Methodism for the enslaved Africans was because of Wesley's ministry among them.[32] The point is that Wesley had firsthand experience with the slave system from his

---

32. Whelchel, "'Chains,'" 103.

experiences in the Americas and in England, and his passion for the slaves' physical and spiritual plight was real.

Indeed, Wesley's theology was orthodox in the sense that relational privileging of a relationship with God was not only right belief but was connected to right behavior and practice or orthopraxis with regard to slavery. Wesley's theology and his evangelical thinking had practical and socio-structural consequences.

Clearly, John Wesley's relevance for the twenty-first century is his conclusion that there is an economics of hope. The hope is in an economy of practical theology that rests human hope clearly in God's present but coming and unfolding rule and reign. Limiting our hope to earning all we can and saving all we can without giving all we can causes us to place our hope in this world rather than in God's unfolding realm. Moreover, to place our hope in this world's economic systems will also cause us to seek our own identity and worth at the expense of others. Thus, a practical theology of the economics of hope in the Wesleyan spirit connects to God's life and God's future.

CHAPTER 6

Practical Public Theology
Civil Rights and the Wesleyan Spirit

ONE OF THE MAJOR characteristics of black Wesleyan practical theology is the refusal to divorce personal salvation from the work of social transformation.[1] Martin Luther King Jr. maintained this tradition of not separating personal and social transformation. This is obvious in his sermon entitled "Transformed Nonconformist."[2] Cecil Wayne Cone also believes liberation theology should not separate personal and social transformation. Moreover, this unity is found in the conversion tradition of African American Christians.[3] This chapter argues that the artificial separation of personal and social transformation undermines the liberational struggle of African Americans. *There is a strong legacy of uniting the personal and social transformation dimensions in African American church history, and it must be recovered if African American practical theology is going to be effective in the twenty-first century.* For too long, liberation theology kept these two dimensions separate, but there is evidence that this alienation is over and that there is a healthy integration of these two dimensions.

Historically, this unity can be seen in the conversion tradition of black Christians in slavery and freedom as well as in the Civil Rights tradition, particularly in the sermons of Dr. Martin Luther King Jr. This chapter explores the Wesleyan and evangelical roots of the Civil

---

1. Whelchel, "'Chains,'" 116–17.
2. King, *Strength*, 10.
3. Cone, *Identity Crisis*.

Rights Movement, particularly in the slave conversion tradition and in selected sermons of Martin Luther King Jr., and gives attention to their presence in black theology. Attention will be given to the rhetorical, practical theological strategies of both Wesley and King. Both remind us that we are citizens of two worlds. There is the world of the "here and now," but there is also the world that is "present and not yet" of God's rule and reign.

The basic theme of this chapter is that the similarity between Wesley and King lay in their rhetoric about living in two worlds. King sought to convince those in the Civil Rights struggle to be "transformed nonconformists."[4] He also asked white Christians to "be not conformed to this world."[5] John Wesley's eighteenth-century rhetoric also addressed the drawback of basing human happiness on this world's riches and, especially, on this world's economic system of slavery and slave trading. His sermons "The Danger of Riches" and "The More Excellent Way" and his treatise "Thoughts Upon Slavery" all addressed the sin of human beings laying up for themselves treasures on earth rather than in the world that was coming but is not yet.[6]

This chapter also explores Anglican and Wesleyan emphasis on evangelism of black people in slavery and its connection to the African American conversion tradition. There was a strong evangelical conversion tradition among black Christians in slavery, which carried over into the early twentieth century and up to the time of the Civil Rights Movement. This presentation links this conversion tradition with King's connection of personal and social transformation.

With regard to the issue of shame, it is clear that the Christian conversion tradition, beginning in slavery and continuing up to the present time, was the source of black people's capacity to deal creatively with the shame and degradation caused by racial oppression and injustice. In fact, it was in the Negro spirituals that it is possible to envisage the connection between social protest, civil rights, justice, and the overcoming of shame. Anne Streaty Wimberly writes:

> The struggle of persons to deal with the trauma of stigmatization and shame is not easy. In truth, it cannot be assumed that black people in slavery did not succumb to their experiences

4. King, *Strength To Love*, 10.
5. Ibid,, 157.
6. Wesley, "Danger," 1–15; "Way," 26–37; and "Thoughts Upon Slavery."

of personal, social, and physical brutalization. In fact, Ronald Salzberger and Mary Turck contend that, for some, the brutalities of slavery resulted in what historian Nell Irvin Painter called "soul murder," insofar as persons experienced an irreversible deadening feeling of self. However, in the very real situation of unspeakable harm faced by black people in slavery, the spirituals were born; and the music attested to the ability of many to overcome shaming attitudes and continue on amidst brutalizing circumstances.[7]

RHETORIC IN THE STORYTELLING OF AFRICAN AMERICANS IN SLAVERY AND FREEDOM

Anglicanism, which was the faith tradition of John Wesley, provided instruction in the Christian faith to enslaved African Americans as early as the mid seventeenth century, but a peculiar thing took place. Early on, black Africans in slavery exercised control over what they learned from the Anglican missionaries. Albert J. Raboteau points out:

> For slaves brought their cultural past to the task of translating and interpreting the doctrinal words and ritual gestures of Christianity. Therefore the meaning which the missionary wished the slaves to receive and the meaning which the slaves actually found (or, better, made) were not the same. The "inaccuracy" of the slaves' translation of Christianity would be a cause of concern to missionaries for a long time to come.[8]

Raboteau continues his emphasis on the freedom slaves enjoyed to interpret and reinterpret Christianity in light of their own African cultural and religious experiences. He also goes on to say that "powerful emotionalism, ecstatic behavior, African dance, and congregational verbal responses were all part of the conversion and evangelical dimension of Protestantism."[9] In short, Raboteau's analysis lays the groundwork for the basic argument of this presentation. That is to say, the similarity between Wesley's use of rhetoric and King's rhetoric in selective sermons and writings lay in American Protestant evangelical revivalism.

It is important to lift up the holistic conversion tradition of black people in slavery and its aftermath. The black conversion tradition

---

7. Wimberly, "Overcoming," 80.
8. Raboteau, *Slave Religion*, 126–27.
9. Ibid., 149.

represents a vast reservoir of orally narrated conversion stories, which were originally told as enslaved people experienced God and received salvation. These conversion experiences of formerly enslaved people were collected in the 1920s and 1930s as researchers interviewed black people who were once enslaved. These orally narrated conversion stories became a rhetorical style of witness taking place within the African American church. It was this tradition that influenced the theology of Martin Luther King Jr. and Cecil Cone.

The conversion tradition was not only an important influence on the thinking of King and on his effort to keep personal and social transformation in dynamic tension: Cecil Wayne Cone sees the conversion tradition of black people in slavery as an important source of black and liberation theology. In contrast to his brother, James Cone, he visualizes the conversion tradition as the source of the essence of black religion and liberation. In short, his work testifies to the holism of the personal and social in addressing oppression.

Cecil Cone's argument in *Identity Crisis in Black Theology* is that it is black peoples' experience of God in the midst of suffering, oppression, slavery, and betrayal that is the source of liberation theology, not Black Power or the Civil Rights Movement.[10] James Cone took the Enlightenment tack of distrusting completely the conversion experience tradition and rooted his theology in the correlation of black theology and liberation theology with Black Power. Cecil Cone argues that black theology should reach back to the history and culture of black people in Africa.[11] For him, it was the conversion tradition growing out of slavery that enabled this African connection.

Cecil Cone says that black religion is "an experience expressed in a confessional story of Black people's relationship with God,"[12] and this is the major source of doing black theology. This experiential understanding of black theology is also the source of the rhetorical thesis of this presentation. I agree with Raboteau's assessment of the convergence of how African Americans in slavery developed their own hermeneutical lenses for interpreting their encounters with God. African tradition gave this conversion tradition its distinctiveness.

---

10. Wimberly, "Significance," 11.
11. Cone, *My Soul Looks Back*, 60.
12. Ibid., 15.

WESLEY AND KING

The conversion tradition of black people in slavery and its aftermath is the source of the holism of personal and social transformation. It is the conversion tradition that provides the link between Wesley and King's emphasis on rhetoric. There is correspondence between the rhetoric of King's "two-world" emphasis and Wesley's "two-world" emphasis. Could Wesley's anti-slavery rhetoric and Kings civil rights rhetoric—in his sermon "Paul's Letter to American Christians"—represent a novel way to transcend political divisions between black Christians and white Christians? Moreover, is it worth pursuing?

Dr. King, in "Paul's Letter to American Christians" in *Strength to Love,* focused on Romans 12:2, and he reminded Christians that we are citizens of two worlds, "the world of time and the world of eternity. Our loyalty, he says, needs to be grounded and rooted in eternity and not in earthly customs and institutions that have fostered slavery, racism, and segregation."[13]

In like manner, Wesley recognizes the danger and limitations of grounding one's identity, worth, happiness, and meaning in this world's promises of riches. Wesley denounced vehemently slave owning and slave trading. His rhetoric not only drew on the notion of choosing the more excellent way, but reached angry emotional levels in trying to convince the slave owner and slave trader that their wellness as human beings was in jeopardy. He also believed slavery blocked God's effort to bring African Americans happiness on earth and in eternity.

WESLEY'S RHETORIC CONTEXT

"Thoughts Upon Slavery," published in the year 1774, shows John Wesley's rhetoric or effort to convince those who forced black people into slave labor and who forcefully removed them from their homes in Africa that bondage and slave trading were contrary the gospel and natural law.[14] This economic system also put the soul of slave traders and owners as well as the souls of those enslaved into mortal danger. His rhetoric was addressed not only to those who were enslaved. It was also directed at the general public as well as the Wesleyan societies or small religious formation groups.

---

13. See Wimberly, *Devotions*, 5.
14. Wesley, "Thoughts."

Wesley's rhetoric was clearly grounded in a theology of happiness. His theology of happiness was based on the belief that true happiness is only in relationship with God and not in the slave system. He tried to convince slave owners and traders that wealth coming out of the system of slavery did not produce glory. He said:

> For first, wealth is not necessary to the glory of any nation; but wisdom, virtue, justice, mercy, generosity, public spirit, love of our country. These are necessary to the real glory of a nation; but abundance of wealth is not."[15]

Wesley also warned the slave owner and trader about the retribution that comes from stealing humans and trading slaves. He said:

> Is there a God? You know there is. Is he a just God? Then there must be a state of retribution; a state wherein the just God will reward every man according to his works. Then what reward will he render to you? O think betimes! Before you drop into eternity! Think now, "He shall have judgment without mercy that showed no mercy."[16]

The point is that according to Wesley's theology laying up for yourselves treasures on earth rather than in the present but coming reign of God led away from true happiness in God and would end in being judged negatively by God.

WESLEY'S RHETORICAL STRATEGIES

What were the familiar rhetorical strategies that John Wesley used to convince people to choose a relationship with God and the world that was unfolding related to God's rule and reign? I have found that many of Wesley's sermons use what is called in modern rhetoric the motivational sequence. The first strategy is to get the attention of those in the audience. The attention-getter is usually a provocative statement such as the following: In Wesley's sermon "The Circumcision of the Heart," which is based on Romans 2:29, Wesley began immediately with the problem he wanted to address in the sermon. He said, "If Christ be risen, ye ought then to die unto the world, and to live wholly unto God."[17] His rhetoric went straight to where he expected the readers and hearers to focus their

15. Ibid.
16. Ibid.
17. Outler and Heitzenrater, *Wesley's Sermons*, 25.

minds and hearts. He wanted them to focus on what it meant to be alive to the world but to be dead to God. Being alive to God involves being renewed by the Spirit of God daily.

After getting the audience's attention, he introduced the problem that he wanted the readers and hearers of the sermon to consider. This was the need to have a circumcised heart, or the testimony, in their hearts, that they were "children of God." As a result, they must give themselves totally to God and not to the desires of this world.[18] His goal was to convince those in the audience that real joy, hope, and happiness began first with a relationship with God. Wesley wrote:

> Let every affection, and thought, and word, and work, be subordinate to this. Whatever ye desire or fear, whatever ye seek or shun, whatever ye think, speak, or do, be it in order to your happiness in God, the sole end as well as source of your being.

He continues:

> Have no end, no ultimate end, but God. Thus our Lord, "One thing is needful." And if thine eye be singly fixed on this one thing, "thy whole body shall be full of light." Thus St. Paul, "This one thing I do; I press toward the mark, after the prize of the high calling in Christ Jesus." Thus St. James, "Cleanse your hands, ye sinners, and purify your hearts, ye double minded." Thus St. John, "Love not the world, neither the things that are in the world. For all that is in the world, the lust of the flesh, the lust of the eye, and the pride of life is not of the Father, but is of the world." The seeking happiness in what gratifies either the desire of the flesh, by agreeably striking upon the outward senses; the desire of the eye, of the imagination, by its novelty, greatness, or beauty; or the pride of life, whether by pomp, grandeur, power, or the usual consequence of them, applause and admiration; "is not of the Father," cometh not from, neither is approved by the Father of spirits; "but of the world;" it is the distinguishing mark of those who will not have him reign over them.[19]

The key point in all of this is what is called rhetorical invention. That is to say that all of Wesley's insight and logic is grounded in the authority of Scripture. Yet, Wesley takes his theology to another level by linking the circumcision of the heart on what he calls "inbred pollution."

---

18. Ibid., 26–27.
19. Ibid., 28–29.

If people are to be perfect, they must add love to their lives, which is the perfection of happiness.[20] Thus, Wesley's rhetoric served the ends of justice, mercy, and love of neighbor. He links personal and social transformation, and it was this linking that eventually led Wesley to condemn slavery and slave trading.

KING'S RHETORICAL CONTEXT

King's rhetorical context and strategies have some major themes in common with John Wesley's. While I am not making a causal link between Wesley and King, I have earlier referred to King's theological understanding of the two-world orientation to time, which grew out of what is called the slave conversion tradition, which was greatly influenced by Anglicanism. Moreover, what King and Wesley had in common was a context that was completely shaped by slavery. Thus, I will say something about the rhetorical context of King as well as his rhetorical strategies.

Dr. Martin Luther King Jr.'s rhetorical context was the Civil Rights Movement period of the 1950s and 1960s. He came to public notoriety because of the Montgomery Bus Boycott of 1955, initiated when Mrs. Rosa Parks violated the official white segregationist bus seating policies, which made it unlawful for a black person to refuse to give up his or her seat for a white person. In fact, by segregationist convention and law, she should have taken a seat in the back of the bus. Her refusal to give up her seat set off a firestorm of reactions among whites and propelled the African American community into one of the most spiritual and human agency actions of protests in United States history.

Dr. Martin Luther King Jr. was pastor of Dexter Avenue Baptist Church and, by his own testimony, indicated that his concern was not about moving off into the prophetic ministry in the pursuit for social justice. His concern was to pastor his church, develop his congregation, and build up the community surrounding his church. Dr. King's intention for this congregation became very clear to me when Dr. Murray Branch—who replaced Dr. King at Dexter Avenue Church and was an Old Testament Professor at the Interdenominational Theological Center—invited me to the now historic Dexter Avenue King Memorial Church to lead that congregation in relational renewal in the late 1970s. It was at that time that I saw Dr. King's strategic plan for the church,

20. Ibid.

and it was clear that he did not intend to address the problems of racial inequality. But it was in the context of segregation, human lynching, and injustice for black people that the Civil Rights Movement was born when Dr. King and Mrs. Rosa Parks answered God's call to action.

KING'S RHETORICAL STRATEGIES

King always had several audiences that he addressed when he preached or wrote his letters. His rhetorical style, like Wesley's, was first to get the audience's attention and then to introduce the problem he would address. After introducing the problem, he would then introduce what he thought would be the solutions, and finally he would help them take actions to solve the problem. I want to briefly examine the rhetorical methods used in two of King's sermons.

The first is "Paul's Letter to American Christians." It was published on November 4, 1956, approximately eleven months after the Montgomery Bus Boycott. His attention-getting method was to draw on a biblical letter-writing genre in the New Testament and to use the rhetorical method of speech-in-character. Speech-in-character is the creative style used to get the attention of others. It either drew on the writer's own biography or on someone else's to cleverly get the message across to the audience.[21] King used the biblical character of the Apostle Paul, knowing that both white and black Christians' attention would be riveted to what would follow.

After completing the customary biblical pattern of an epistolary greeting, King contemporized his letter and made it speak to the modern situation. He did this by referring to the advances in science and the marvels of technology. Yet, he suddenly turned to focus on the lack of human progress in the moral and spiritual area. After giving specifics of the inability to foster brother and sisterhood and progress in war, he went to the heart of the problem he wanted to address. This problem is what he called giving "ultimate allegiance to man-made systems and customs."[22] He went on to say:

> American Christians, I must say to you what I wrote to the Roman Christians years ago: "Be not conformed to this world, but be ye transformed by the renewing of your mind." You have

---

21. Jewett, *Romans*, 1019.
22. King Jr., *Strength*, 157.

> a dual citizenry. You live both in time and eternity. Your highest loyalty is to God, and not to the mores or the folkways, the state or the nation, or any man-made institution. If any earthly institution or custom conflicts with God's will, it is your Christian duty to oppose it. You must never allow the transitory, evanescent demands of man-made institutions to take precedence over the eternal demands of the Almighty God.[23]

King also returns to this theme of belonging to two worlds in the sermon "Transformed Nonconformist." Here, he also talked about the same theme that Wesley trumpeted often, and this theme was happiness. Wesley and King's rhetoric had the same source: the gospel of Jesus Christ. King wrote: "When an affluent society would coax us to believe that happiness consists in the size of our automobiles, the impressiveness of our houses, and the expensiveness of our cloths, Jesus reminds us, 'A man's life consisteth not in the abundance of the things which he possesseth.'"[24]

The similarity of Wesley and King's theology rested in their common understanding of the time dualism that was Pauline to the core. We live in two worlds. We live in the world of now and the world that is present but not yet; it is coming, and it is where God will reign and rule. Jesus inaugurated the coming of the new age, and God will complete it at the end of time.

It was indicated earlier that the common source of this time orientation to the two worlds came from Anglican missionary emphases. Wesley spent several years in the American colonies during slavery, and he befriended many persons who were in slavery. This experience as well as his knowledge of slave trading in Britain eventually led to his anti-slavery effort.

Those persons in slavery took what the missionaries preached and taught and transformed it into a message and strategy that would eventually lead them out of slavery. King built on this tradition, and added non-violent protest to it, to fashion the Civil Rights Movement. His loyalty was always to the vision that he saw growing out of Paul's theology, that we must be committed to the world that is coming rather than to this world's riches and human-made customs.

---

23. Ibid., 157–58.
24. Ibid., 11.

THE CIVIL RIGHTS MOVEMENT AND BLACK POWER: A BRIDGE TO PERSONAL AND SOCIAL TRANSFORMATION

I was never convinced that the wedge driven between personal and social transformation was as wide as some in the Black Power Movement indicated. My theological mentor was James Deotis Roberts, and his theology became the theological underpinning of my doctoral dissertation, which I defended in November of 1975, while in my first year of teaching at ITC. I was very happy when Cecil Cone's book appeared in 1975 as well, because it also confirmed that the wedge between personal and social transformation was artificial in black theology.

Cecil asked me to write a brief statement endorsing the revised edition of his book *The Identity Crisis in Black Theology*, which appeared in 2003.[25] I was more than delighted to write something, since his work had given me courage to say what I had to say about social and personal transformation and about conversion. In my statement, I said the following about Cecil's book:

> In summary, *The Identity Crisis in Black Theology* is a forerunner to post-Enlightenment theology. It trusts our experience as African American Christians with God in the midst of suffering. From the experience, we draw hope and courage from God to resist enslavement, to overcome racism, sexism, classism, homophobia, and ageism, as well as strength to resist being recruited into negative identities. Moreover, our experience with God enables us to become co-workers in liberating others from oppression.[26]

What struck me as significant also was James Cone's embrace of the personal dimension of transformation in his book *Risks of Faith*. In it he becomes transparent about his upbringing in Macedonia AME Church in Bearden, Arkansas.[27] He said:

> Every Sunday and sometimes on weeknights I encountered Jesus through rousing sermons, fervent prayers, spirited gospel songs, and the passionate testimonies of the people. Jesus was the dominant reality at Macedonia and in black life in Bearden. The people walked with him and told him about their troubles as if he were a trusted friend who understood their trails and tribulations in this unfriendly world.

---

25. Cone, *Identity*, 11–12.
26. Ibid., 12.
27. Cone, *Risks*, ix.

He continued:

> Like the people of Macedonia, Jesus became a significant presence in my life, too. I do not remember the exact date or time I "turned to Jesus," as the conversion experience was called. At home, church, and school, at play and at work, Jesus was always there, as the anchor of life, giving it meaning and purpose and bestowing hope and faith in the ultimate justice to things. Jesus was that reality who empowered black people to know that they were not worthless human beings that white people said they were.[28]

In 1999, there was no longer a division between James and Cecil. Personal transformation and social transformation were linked as they were for Wesley and King. What is of more significance as well was that the Anglican and Wesleyan missionary influence enabled black people in slavery to fashion their own understanding of Jesus and God and their presence in their lives to inform their theology. With this convergence between King and Wesley and the Cone brothers, the next section will explore the implications of this rhetorical and theological correspondence for practical theology.

IMPLICATIONS: PRACTICAL THEOLOGY IN CIVIL RIGHTS AND WESLEYAN SPIRIT

The rhetorical strategies of Wesley and King have implications for practical theology in the Civil Rights and Wesleyan spirit, which will be developed. The thrust of the implications will be a model of narrative and strategic theology that holds in tension evangelism, narrative therapy, nurturance, and public theology.

Practical theology from a narrative frame is all about helping people with whom we are ministering to identify the major metanarratives at work within their immediate meaning-making context. Metanarratives are those dominant story plots existing within people's meaning-making context that compete for people's allegiance and influence their choices. We have established that Wesley and King adopted a biblical and theological frame that envisages the world as being made up of two distinct levels, which are a this-world-oriented metanarrative and one oriented with the present-but-not-yet, coming rule and reign of God.

---

28. Ibid., x.

Understanding reality in light of these two competing worldviews has all kinds of limitations. I will name two. The first limitation is that all metanarratives are social constructions by those who are in power and have the ability to persuade people, through coercive or non-coercive means, to choose their conception of reality. This is the deconstructive postmodern critique. That is to say that we need to be suspicious of all metanarratives, because they are formed as the result of the powerful people in culture.

A second limitation is the argument that posing two separate metanarratives is a dualistic conception of reality, which is out of step with modern holistic conceptions of reality. One is spiritual and the other is material.

My response is that all conceptions of reality are social constructions of reality, but it is impossible for human beings, no matter how intelligent we are, to live without metanarratives. Given this understanding of human finiteness, I opt for a Pauline view of reality, which Wesley and King embraced. A Pauline dualism is an eschatological time dualism, and it is related to past, present, and future time dimensions. All human metanarratives are social constructions using time-oriented analogies and emphases. Moreover, no thinker has found ways to transcend time categories in conceptualizing reality.

Power is very much a factor in the development of metanarratives. This was no less the case in the slave conversion tradition or in the theology of Martin Luther King Jr. There is, however, one major difference between the metanarratives developed by oppressors and those that came from black people in slavery and its aftermath. The metanarratives of the powerful come from alliance to an idolatry of this world's values, and these values indicate that it is possible to gain identity, happiness, economic prosperity, and wellbeing at the expense of others. Black people in slavery and its aftermath—especially in the conversion experiences of black people in slavery and its aftermath—did not find their source of power in the world or in themselves. Rather, they found their power in God and in God's present but coming rule and reign in this world. This metanarrative was not an expression built on the backs of others through oppression and exploitation. No, it was rather a metanarrative that came from their relationship with God and God's present but not yet rule and reign. This relationship with God was the source of their agency and power to speak to the forces of evil and oppression in this world.

Practical theology from a narrative frame is all about the ecclesiology and the task to persuade people to choose the present-but-not-yet eschatological plot, which in the eyes of Wesley, King, and the Cone brothers includes all facets of ministry in degrees of emphasis. My own critical emphasis, however, focuses on the need to recover the village functions of the small group, primarily because of what Cornell West calls cultural nihilism. Cultural nihilism is based on the reality that the mediating structures that stand between human beings and the wider structures of society have collapsed, such as the family, extended family, voluntary associations, small groups, networks, and fellowships. The result has been the loss of love, the loss of meaning, and the loss of purpose.[29] This means that practical theological strategies, including public theological strategies, need to target the use of mediating structures as the venues and arenas for helping people make decisions about the choice between two plot narratives.

DECONSTRUCTING METANARRATIVES

The basic premise of the narrative approach to practical theology is that all metanarratives must be deconstructed so that they focus on God's present and coming world of reality rather than on the this-world orientation. The deconstructive rhetoric must focus on those who promote oppression as well as those who are the victims of oppression. In narrative practical theology, the strategies for deconstruction are externalization and internalization. Externalization is the process of helping people, whether victims or perpetrators of oppression, to examine their beliefs and convictions about themselves, their relationships with others, and their relationship with God.[30] Internalization is helping people examine the convictions and beliefs that they have internalized or into which they have been recruited by those who are oppressors.[31]

Externalization is a rhetorical process wherein people are asked a series of questions designed to help them reflect on their deeply held convictions. For example, for oppressors these questions would begin with how they as human beings first established their identities in life. These questions would include issues such as those related to when they

---

29. West, *Race Matters*.
30. Wimberly, *Recalling Our Own Stories*.
31. Wimberly, *Counseling and Care*.

learned that status, position, power, wealth, and social standing were important, and how essential these dimensions are for their happiness, identity, and wellbeing. A second focus for the oppressor is whether or not it is acceptable to use others as means to the ends of achieving happiness, identity, wellbeing, and worth in life.

After these questions are answered, the next series of questions would involve whether or not strategies of gaining identity have actually been effective in achieving happiness, identity, worth, and dignity. Here, the focus is on trying to help those who have established their identities at the expense of others to assess whether they are really happy and fulfilled. The criteria for doing this kind of evaluation is whether or not those involved feel that there is something missing in their lives.

For victims of oppression, the questions are different. The questions have to do with those convictions and beliefs about themselves that resulted from being coerced and recruited into negative identities. These convictions and beliefs are explored by exploring themes and feelings related to social status, self-esteem, value, worth, honor versus shame, and self-regard. The key is to help people speak out loud or externalize these convictions and beliefs about themselves and others and to access whether or not they are happy or satisfied with them. Following this, then, the focus is on what to do with these beliefs and convictions.

Whether one is an oppressor or a victim of oppression, the key is to re-author or re-edit the metanarratives or beliefs and convictions that one holds about oneself. Key in this process is the discernment of what God is doing in one's life to update one's metanarrative. Indeed, the focus is on the fact that God cares about whether the metanarrative is oriented toward this-world values and how those values lead to self and other destruction. Indeed, God desires our wellbeing and happiness and knows that the source of our ultimate happiness is the metanarrative oriented toward the world that is present but still coming. Our happiness is in being grounded in God and God's future.

CONCLUSION

The basic argument of this concluding chapter is that personal and social transformation, of human beings and of society, are key emphases that we must recover in the twenty-first-century practical theology. Keeping these two dimensions apart distorts reality and makes it difficult to make an impact on human behavior and on social structures. The rhetorical ideas of John Wesley and Martin Luther King Jr. were drawn on as examples of how rhetoric can be used to foster personal and social transformation and to hold them in creative tension. Moreover, both the conversion tradition of black people, in slavery and freedom, and the reconciliation between James and Cecil Cone, in their thinking about personal and social transformation, also speak to the clear necessity of holding these two dimensions in tension. The conclusion is that human happiness requires human beings to attend to their personal relationships with God as well as their relationships to others and to social institutions and structures. One without the other prevents true personal and social transformation. Moreover, overcoming shame begins first in our relationship with God, and from that starting point, we begin to construct relational and ethical responses concerned with our neighbor and our neighbor's wellbeing. Through our relationship with God and with others shame can be overcome.

Bibliography

Ayers, Jeremy. "John Wesley's Therapeutic Understanding of Salvation." *Encounter* 63:3 (summer 2002) 263–97.
The Book of Discipline of The United Methodist Church 2008. Nashville: The United Methodist Publishing House, 2008.
Browning, Don S. *Religious Thought and the Modern Psychologies*. Philadelphia: Fortress, 1987.
Campbell, Ted A. "John Wesley as Diarist and Correspondent." In *The Cambridge Companion to John Wesley*, edited by Randy L. Maddox and Jason E. Vickers. New York: Cambridge University Press, 2010.
Carey, Brycchan. "John Wesley's *Thoughts Upon Slavery* and the Language of the Heart." *The Bulletin of the John Rylands University Library of Manchester* 85:2–3 (summer/autumn 2003).
Charry, Ellen. *By the Renewing of Your Minds: The Pastoral Function of Christian Doctrine*. New York: Oxford University Press, 1997.
Clark, J. C. D. "Changes in the Received Model of the Eighteenth Century." In *The Oxford Handbook of Methodist Studies*, edited by William J. Abraham and James E. Kirby. New York: Oxford University Press, 2009.
Cone, Cecil Wayne. *Identity Crisis in Black Theology*. Rev. ed. Nashville: AMEC, 2003.
Cone, James. *My Soul Looks Back: Journeys in Faith*. Nashville: Abingdon, 1982.
———. *Risks of Faith: The Emergence of a Black Theology of Liberation, 1968–1998*. Boston: Beacon, 1999.
Dodd, C. H. *Parables of the Kingdom*. New York: Scribner, 1961.
Ellingsen, Mark. *The Integrity of Biblical Narrative: Story in Theology and Proclamation*. Minneapolis: Fortress, 1990.
———. *Reclaiming Our Roots: Martin Luther to Martin Luther King*. Harrisburg, PA: Trinity International, 1999.
Frank, Thomas Edward. "Discipline." In *The Oxford Handbook of Methodist Studies*, edited by William J. Abraham and James E. Kirby, 245–61. New York: Oxford University Press, 2009.
Franklin, Robert M. *Another Day's Journey: Black Churches Confronting the American Crisis*. Minneapolis: Fortress, 1997.
———. "Travelin Shoes: Resources for Our Journey." *Journal of the Interdenominational Theological Center* 25:1 (fall 1997) 3.
Gardiner, William. "O God, My God, My All Thou Art!" Translated by John Wesley. No pages. Online: http://www.cyberhymnal.orghtm/o/g/m/ogmgmatta.htm.

Goldberg, Michael. *Theology and Narrative: A Critical Introduction.* Nashville: Abingdon, 1982.
Gregory, Jeremy. "The Long Eighteenth Century." In *The Cambridge Companion to John Wesley*, edited by Randy L. Maddox and Jason E. Vickers. New York: Cambridge University Press, 2010.
Harris, Frederick C. *Something Within: Religion in African American Activism.* New York: Oxford University Press, 1999.
Heitzenrater, Richard P. "The Poor and the People Called Methodists, 1729–1999." In *The Poor and the People Called Methodist*, edited by Richard P. Heitzenrater, 15–38. Nashville: Kingswood, 2002.
Hempton, David N. "Wesley in Context." In *The Cambridge Companion to John Wesley*, edited by Randy L. Maddox and Jason E. Vickers, 60–78. New York: Cambridge University Press, 2010.
Henderson, Glenn. *Treasures of Darkness: Prelude to Prosperity.* Atlanta: GH Group, 2009.
Hunter, Rodney J., ed. *Dictionary of Pastoral Care and Counseling.* Exp. ed. Nashville: Abingdon, 2005.
Jennings, Theodore W., Jr. *Good News to the Poor: John Wesley's Evangelical Economics.* Nashville: Abingdon, 1990.
Jewett, Robert. *Romans: A Commentary.* Minneapolis: Fortress, 2007.
King, Martin Luther, Jr. *Strength to Love.* New York: Harper and Row, 1963.
Lawton, George. *John Wesley's English: A Study of His Literary Style.* London: Allen & Unwin, 1962.
Lovin, Robin. "Human Rights, Vocation, and Human Dignity." In *Our Calling to Fulfill: Wesley's Views on the Church in Mission*, edited by M. Douglas Meeks, 109–23. Nashville: Kingwood, 2009.
Maddox, Randy L. *Responsible Grace: John Wesley's Practical Theology.* Nashville: Kingswood, 1994.
———. "Theology of John and Charles Wesley." In *T&T Clark Companion to Methodism*, edited by Charles Yrigoyen Jr., 20–35. New York: T. & T. Clark International, 2010.
Marquardt, Manfred. *John Wesley's Social Ethics: Praxis and Principles.* Translated by John E. Steely and W. Stephen Gunter. Nashville: Abingdon, 1992.
———. "Social Ethics in Methodist Tradition." In *T&T Clark Companion to Methodism*, edited by Charles Yrigoyen Jr., 292–308. New York: T. & T. Clark International, 2010.
May, Herbert G., and Bruce Metzger, eds. *The New Oxford Annotated Bible: Revised Standard Version.* Oxford: Oxford University Press, 1973.
Meeks, M. Douglas. "A Home for the Homeless: Vocation, Mission, and Church in Wesleyan Perspective." In *Our Calling to Fulfill: Wesleyan Views of the Church in Mission*, edited by M. Douglas Meeks, 1–10. Nashville: Kingswood, 2009.
Melton, J. Gordon. *A Will to Choose: The Origins of African American Methodism.* New York: Rowman & Littlefield, 2007.
Miles, Rebekah L. "Happiness, Holiness, and the Moral in John Wesley." In *The Cambridge Companion to John Wesley*, edited by Randy L. Maddox and Jason E. Vickers, 207–24. New York: Cambridge University Press, 2010.
Moore, Mary Elizabeth. "The United Methodist Church at 40: What Can We Hope For?" *Methodist Review: Journal of Wesleyan and Methodist Studies*, vol. 1, (2009): 69–91. Online: http://www.methodistreview.org/

Niebuhr, H. Richard. *The Meaning of Revelation*. New York: Macmillan, 1941.
Patton, John. *Is Human Forgiveness Possible: A Pastoral Care Perspective*. 1985. Reprint, Nashville: Abingdon, 2003.
Raboteau, Albert J. *Slave Religion: The "Invisible Institution" in the Antebellum South*. New York: Oxford University Press, 1978.
Richardson, Alan, and John Bowden, eds. *The Westminster Dictionary of Christian Theology*. Philadelphia: Westminster, 1983.
Richey, Russell E., et al. *Marks of Methodism: Theology in Ecclesial Practice* Nashville: Abingdon, 2005.
Rivers, Isabel. *Reason, Grace and Sentiment: A Study of the Language of Religion and Ethics in England, 1660–1780*. Vol. 1. New York: Cambridge University Press, 1991.
Runyon, Theodore. "Orthopathy: Wesleyan Criteria for Religious Experience." In *"Heart Religion" in the Methodist Tradition and Related Movements*, edited by Richard B. Steele. Lanham, MD: Scarecrow, 2001.
Smith, Warren Thomas. *John Wesley and Slavery*. Nashville: Abingdon, 1986.
Suchocki, Marjarie. "Wesleyan Grace." In *Oxford Handbook of Methodist Studies*, edited by William Abraham and James E. Kirby, 540–53. New York: Oxford University Press, 2010.
Thomas, Rebecca, and Stephen Parker. "Toward a Theological Understanding of Shame." *Journal of Psychology and Christianity* 23:2 (summer 2004) 176–82.
Tillich, Paul. *The Courage to Be*. New Haven: Yale University Press, 1952.
Twenge, Jean M., and W. Keith Campbell. *The Narcissism Epidemic: Living in the Entitlement*. New York: Free Press, 2009.
Whelchel, L. Henry, Jr. "'My Chains Fell Off': Heart Religion in the African American Methodist Tradition." In *"Heart Religion" in the Methodist Tradition and Related Movements*, edited by Richard B. Steele, 97–125. Lanham, MD: Scarecrow, 2001.
Wesley, John. "The Danger of Riches." In *The Works of John Wesley*, vol. 7, 1–15. Grand Rapids: Baker, 1998.
———. "John Wesley's Explanatory Notes on the Whole Bible Commentary." No pages. Online: www.biblestudytools.com/commentaries/wesleys-explanatory-notes
———. "John Wesley's Notes on the Bible." 1704. Online: www.biblestudyguide.org/ebooks/comment/Wesley-notes.pdf.
———. *John Wesley's Sermons: An Anthology*. Edited by Albert C. Outler and Richard P. Heitzenrater. Nashville: Abingdon, 1991.
———. *Journals and Diaries*. Edited by W. Reginald Ward and Richard P. Heitzenrater. Vols. 18–24 of *The Works of John Wesley: The Bicentennial Edition*. Nashville: Abingdon, 1976.
———. "On Dress." In *Sermons*, edited by Albert C. Outler. Vols. 1–4 of *The Works of John Wesley: The Bicentennial Edition*. Nashville: Abingdon, 1976.
———. "On Public Diversions." In *Sermons*, edited by Albert C. Outler. Vols. 1–4 of *The Works of John Wesley: The Bicentennial Edition*. Nashville: Abingdon, 1976.
———. "On Worldly Folly." In *Sermons*, edited by Albert C. Outler. Vols. 1–4 of *The Works of John Wesley: The Bicentennial Edition*. Nashville: Abingdon, 1976.
———. "The More Excellent Way." In *Sermons*, edited by Albert C. Outler. Vols. 1–4 of *The Works of John Wesley: The Bicentennial Edition*. Nashville: Abingdon, 1976.
———. *Sermons*. Edited by Albert C. Outler. Vols. 1–4 of *The Works of John Wesley: The Bicentennial Edition*. Nashville: Abingdon, 1976.

———. "Thoughts Upon Slavery." 1774. No pages. Online: http://gbgm-umc.org/umw/wesley/thoughtsuponslavery.stm.

———. *The Works of John Wesley.* Vol. 8. Grand Rapids: Baker, 1998.

West, Cornell. *Race Matters.* New York: Vintage, 1993.

White, Michael. *Re-Authoring Lives: Interviews and Essays.* Adelaide, South Australia: Dulwich Centre Publications, 1998.

Wimberly, Anne Streaty. "Overcoming Shame in Slave Songs and the Epistle to the Hebrews." In *The Shame Factor: How Shame Shapes Society,* edited by Robert Jewett. Eugene, OR: Cascade, 2011.

Wimberly, Edward P. *African American History Month Daily Devotions.* Nashville: Abingdon, 2008.

———. *African American Pastoral Care and Counseling: The Politics of Oppression and Empowerment.* Cleveland: Pilgrim, 2006.

———. "The Bible as Pastor: An African American Perspective." *The Journal of Pastoral Theology* 16:1 (spring 2006) 63–80.

———. "John Wesley and the Twenty-First Century: A Realistic Future." *Methodist Review: A Journal of Wesleyan and Methodist Studies* 1 (2009) 93–107. Online: http://www.methodistreview.org.

———. *Moving From Shame to Self-Worth: Preaching and Pastoral Care.* Nashville: Abingdon, 1999.

———. "No Shame in Wesley's Gospel." In *The Shame Factor: How Shame Shapes Society,* edited by Robert Jewett. Eugene, OR: Cascade, 2011.

———. *Recalling Our Own Stories: Spiritual Renewal for Religious Caregivers.* San Francisco: Jossey-Bass, 1997.

———. *Relational Refugees: Alienation and Reincorporation in African American Churches and Communities.* Nashville: Abingdon, 2000.

———. "The Significance of the Work of Cecil Wayne Cone." In *The Identity Crisis in Black Theology,* by Cecil Wayne Cone. Nashville: AMEC, 2003.

———. *Using Scripture in Pastoral Counseling.* Nashville: Abingdon, 1994.

Wurmser, Leon. *The Mask of Shame.* Northvale, NJ: Jason Aronson, 1994.

www.ingramcontent.com/pod-product-compliance
Lightning Source LLC
Chambersburg PA
CBHW071502160426
43195CB00013B/2187